Strangest of All

FRANK EDWARDS

A Carol Paperbacks Book
Published by Carol Publishing Group

TO

MY MOTHER

First Carol Paperbacks Edition 1991

Copyright © 1956, 1984 by Frank Edwards

A Carol Paperbacks Book
Published by Carol Publishing Group

Editorial Offices   Sales & Distribution Offices
600 Madison Avenue   120 Enterprise Avenue
New York, NY 10022   Secaucus, NJ 07094

In Canada: Musson Book Company
A Division of General Publishing Co. Limited
Don Mills, Ontario

Carol Paperbacks is a registered trademark of
Carol Communications, Inc.

Queries regarding rights and permissions
should be addressed to: Carol Publishing Group,
600 Madison Avenue, New York, NY 10022

Manufactured in the United States of America
ISBN 0-8216-2504-7

10 9 8 7 6 5 4 3 2 1

Carol Publishing Group books are available at special discounts
for bulk purchases, for sales promotions, fund raising, or
educational purposes. Special editions can also be created to
specifications. For details contact: Special Sales Department,
Carol Publishing Group, 120 Enterprise Ave., Secaucus, NJ 07094

Contents

Contents

Introduction

This is my private collection of curious classics.

The strange footprints that plagued the good folk of Devonshire a century ago are matched by the carefully measured and photographed footprints of the Abominable Snowmen of our own time. The bewildering disappearance of Oliver Larch is no more puzzling than that of more than a score of modern military and commercial planes which have mutely flown into a small section of the Atlantic near the east coast of the U.S.A. What their fate was we do not know, for no passenger has returned from his unknown, unmarked grave. The astounding capabilities of the Elberfeld horses are equalled if not exceeded by the remarkable Lady Wonder of Richmond, Virginia. Marconi, hunched over his crude apparatus at the turn of the century, was certain that he was recording signals from Mars. Fifty years later scientists in scores of great observatories are engaged in a similar project. Like Marconi, they are unable to explain what they are receiving —or its origin.

In this book I have set down the details of many such stories.

Each of them was headline news in its own time; some of them are still news today. They are stories that will start many arguments but never conclude one, because they are stories for which there are no ready answers.

Here they are on the record—living proof that the age of mystery never ends.

FRANK EDWARDS

The Equine Wizards of Elberfeld

If Wilhelm Von Osten was right, the world has been making a tragic error for countless centuries, for Von Osten was a staunch believer in the incredible intelligence of animals. It was his contention that many animals, and especially horses, are capable of intellectual attainments far beyond the normal limits ascribed to them. That they fail to reach this development is due to man's folly, in Von Osten's opinion.

Wilhelm, free' to pursue his obsession by virtue of a small inheritance, annoyed his fellow townsmen by bouncing uninvited into their conversations to bombard them with his favourite topic. Berlin soon came to regard him as an eccentric, which is putting it mildly.

In order to prove that dumb animals were dumb only because they had not had the advantages of higher education, Wilhelm had to come up with some evidence. His modest income did not permit of any sizable expenditures, so it is not surprising that his first trainee, so to speak, was an ancient and ailing circus bear which he bought for next to nothing.

Whether the bear was harbouring some hidden intelligence will never be known. Wilhelm's landlord objected to the bear's living in the humble quarters which Wilhelm had rented only for himself. The neighbours objected on the ground that the bear possessed more odour than brains. They also objected, and not unreasonably, to Wilhelm's habit of shouting at the bear at the top of his voice at all hours of the day and night. Hour after hour, he would bellow, *'one!—two!—three!'* The beleaguered Bruin seemed to take no interest in this annoying rumpus other than to growl menacingly when Wilhelm accented his fundamentals of arithmetic by clouting the bear on the head with a roll of newspaper. Obviously this sort of thing had to stop before the teacher got beyond 'four'—and stop it did.

Apparently one of the disgruntled neighbours slipped into Von Osten's room in his absence and unchained the pupil. At least this was Von Osten's complaint. Be that as it may, he did not stay long in the room upon his return. Bear and teacher came down the stairway in a dead heat, taking their leave of each other at the street with mutual relief.

We should not dismiss the possibility that the unfortunate bear in this case might have been deaf, and there can be little doubt that he was allergic to arithmetic to the tune of a rolled-up newspaper. Herr Von Osten, who was best qualified to judge the case, never again tried to teach any animals except horses, and judging from the results it was a very sound decision.

His first equine student was on a mental par with the bear. After several months of patience-straining endeavours, Wilhelm sent the horse back into circulation in the capacity for which it seemed so well equipped: that of hauling a small cart for a vegetable farmer.

Von Osten began his experiments with the bear in 1895 and followed that ill-starred venture with the cart-horse in 1896. For four years thereafter he seems to have devoted his time to lively, if one-sided, discussions of the subject with anyone who would listen. Then, in 1896, Von Osten came into possession of the horse that was to mark a turning-point in his life.

Hans was a Russian stallion, young, beautiful and intelligent. Under the intensive tutelage of Wilhelm Von Osten, Hans made such rapid progress that he soon acquired the prefix 'Kluge' (clever), and Clever Hans seems to have richly merited the title.

If the horse had latent intelligence that needed only training and some method of expression to bring it to full fruition, Von Osten was willing and eager to devote himself to the task. He first familiarized Hans with such common ideas as top, bottom, right, left—tapping the objects under discussion to emphasize his teaching. As soon as Kluge Hans got the idea and could respond by touching the proper side to indicate that he understood, Von Osten advanced from these simple symbols to elementary arithmetic.

On a table before the horse he placed one small object, in the first case a skittle. Repeating over and over, 'one—one—one,' he taught the horse to paw one time with his hoof each time he heard the word 'one' or saw one object on the table. Von Osten says that it took about a month to teach Clever Hans to count up to four. After that the progress was surprisingly rapid. The objects were replaced by figures on a blackboard, for Von Osten believed that the horse would be able to understand that numerals represented objects and sounds. The results seem to indicate that he was right.

The name and fame of Clever Hans spread rapidly and it was inevitable that he should attract the attention of scholars. One such was Professor E. Clarapede of the University of Geneva who spent weeks observing and testing the remarkable stallion. In his report on the subject Professor Clarapede says:

'Hans could do more than mere sums: he knew how to read; he could (also) distinguish between harmonious and dissonant chords of music. He also had an extraordinary memory: he could tell the date of each day of the current week. In short, he got through all the tasks which an intelligent schoolboy of fourteen is able to perform.'

Among other things, Professor Clarapede posed oral and written problems in cube root (solutions unknown to anyone who was present), and in every instance Kluge Hans pawed out the correct answers without hesitation. The savant noticed that Hans was invariably correct if he tapped out the answers instantaneously;

if he hesitated, as though to think about it, he was generally wrong. In this respect, Professor Clarapede noted, the famed Elberfeld horse resembled the human prodigies who could work out complicated mathematical problems mentally. They, too, had to deal with the problems quickly and intuitively in order to arrive at the correct answers.

As the story of Clever Hans spread far and wide throughout Europe, visitors flocked from everywhere to see this living confirmation of Von Osten's theory of animal intelligence. And, as might be expected, Clever Hans soon became the centre of bitter controversy.

Some learned observers flatly branded him a fraud and his performance a clever bit of fakery. Other observers, equally as eminent, defended the horse and his owner as genuine and credible. There the matter stood until 1904, when a scientific committee was appointed to resolve this matter once and for all. Professors of psychology, physiology, zoology and medicine were included, along with a circus manager, two cavalry officers and a trio of veterinarians. This group spent five weeks examining, contemplating, considering and observing the antics of this remarkable stallion, finally retiring to their respective bases to decide what they had seen. Their report set down their experiences in factual manner: they had seen the horse do some complicated mathematical problems which they themselves had submitted. The horse had tapped out replies to questions. He exhibited an amazing ability to perform feats which indicated intelligence far beyond that generally conceded to the equine world. If the horse's abilities were genuine, it was astounding; if they were fraudulent, it was a remarkably clever trick. Smart horse or clever fraud? The committee could only report that it had found much to startle its members and nothing to arouse their suspicions—but it offered no definitive conclusion.

Obviously, with several important newspapers out on the limb denouncing the horse as a fraud, this sort of committee action could not be tolerated. A second committee was appointed, including on its roster the name of Oskar Pfungst, head of a

Berlin psychological laboratory and a man whose low opinion of Clever Hans was no secret. Though Mr. Pfungst was biased, he was also eminent and anything he had to say would carry a great deal of authority.

After this second study of Kluge Hans, Herr Pfungst had much to say, so much in fact that it constituted a book entitled *Clever Hans* which appeared on the market in 1912. The gist of this tome is that Clever Hans was just that—so clever that he had fooled other highly intelligent investigators, but not clever enough to deceive Herr Pfungst. It has been described as a voluminous and crushing report and it was admittedly all of that. In it Herr Pfungst declared that Clever Hans had no intelligence beyond that of any ordinary horse, did not know how to calculate or count, and recognized neither letters nor figures. In short, he regarded Hans as a fugitive from a dray wagon, earning his living and that of his master by perpetrating a colossal fraud.

How was this done? Herr Pfungst emphatically stated that it was all done by getting the horse to obey signs from Von Osten, subtle movements and shadings of voice which gave Hans the cue for his 'replies'.

This blast from such a prominent figure as Herr Pfungst created doubt in the minds of many who had been convinced, it created conviction in the minds where there had been doubt. Public opinion veered away from Von Osten and his equine friend. He tried in vain to secure a less biased probe but no one in public life cared to fly in the face of Herr Pfungst's blockbuster. Frustrated, lonely and embittered, Wilhelm Von Osten died in June of 1909 at the age of seventy-one.

But for one man, the work and theories of Von Osten might have died with him. That one man was a wealthy manufacturer of Elberfeld, Herr Krall, who had taken a considerable interest in Von Osten's work and to whom Kluge Hans was transferred by Von Osten's will. Krall had upon occasion conducted some experiments on the horse while Von Osten lived. Now that the horse was his by inheritance, Krall decided to devote even more of his time to the enigmatic creature.

Krall was a kindly, quiet man who never lost his temper or his patience in dealing with his pupil. This was in marked contrast to the gesticulating and irascible Von Osten. Under the tutelage of Krall, Hans expanded his abilities and became a more reliable student, less given to the caprices which had so frequently exasperated his original owner. There were no longer any of those mental collisions between horse and master. Instead there developed a distinct fondness between the two, Krall and Hans, which was instantly recognized by all who saw them at work.

After the public denunciation by Pfungst, interest in the performance of Hans diminished rapidly. This was actually a help to Krall, for it gave him ample time to devote to his pet project without the handicap of an audience. He bought two fine Arabian stallions, Muhamed and Zarif, to add to his pupil, for Krall had some ideas of his own and wished to ascertain whether he too could develop the latent mental abilities of horses, starting from scratch.

Maurice Maeterlinck, who spent considerable time at Elberfeld with Krall and his horses, describes the scene:

> 'Krall . . . adores his pupils; and in this atmosphere of affection has in a manner of speaking humanized them. There are no longer those sudden movements of wild panic which reveal the ancestral dread of man in the quietest and best trained horse. He talks to them long and tenderly, as a father might talk to his children; and we have the strange feeling that they listen to all he says and understand it. If they appear not to grasp an explanation or a demonstration, he will begin it all over again, analyse it, paraphrase it ten times in succession, with the patience of a mother.'

Under this type of tutelage the progress of the Arabian stallions was much swifter than that of Hans. Within two weeks of the first lesson, says Maeterlinck, Muhamed was doing small problems in arithmetic correctly. He had learned to distinguish the tens from the units, we are told, striking the tens with his left hoof and the units with the right. He appears to have known the meaning of the plus and minus symbols. Eighteen days after his first lesson Muhamed was ready for introduction to multiplication and division of small numbers. Maeterlinck and others have recorded that after four months' teaching by Krall, Muhamed could extract square and cube roots; a few months later he was taught to spell and to read by means of an unusual alphabet devised by Krall. This consisted of a system whereby the horse indicated the letters of the alphabet by tapping alternately with his front feet. While it sounds complicated, it was in reality nothing more than a form of Morse code with one foot representing the dots and the other the dashes. The astounding part of the matter is that it was being taught to a horse and that the horse reportedly grasped and used it.

The progress of Muhamed was little short of remarkable, and he soon exceeded the famed exploits of his predecessor, Kluge Hans. Of the other Arabian stallion, Zarif, it can be said that his progress was also notable although he seemed to be less gifted than Muhamed, especially in the field of higher mathematics.

After about six months of training under the inspired Herr Krall, this equine trio was attracting thousands of visitors. They were admitted without charge, for Krall wished to be free of any suspicion that he was using the horses for pecuniary gain; he had ample personal funds, and training these horses was a hobby which he could easily afford, although it took a toll of his health. His efforts to train Hänschen, a Shetland pony, were as frustrating and unrewarding as the time he spent with Kama, a baby elephant. After months of patient effort on his part, Krall had to admit that neither of these diminutive pupils showed any interest in anything more than feeding time. 'Lovable,' he said of them, 'but just pets, nothing more.'

But the fantastic attainments of his three principal stars were enough to make his cup run over. They tapped out replies to questions from thousands of visitors. They performed feats of higher mathematics for learned men from the principal universities of Europe: Sarasin of Basle; Beredka of Pasteur

B

Institute; Schoeller and Gehrke of Berlin; Mackenzie of Genoa; Ferrari of Bologna, and many others who came to witness and to wonder.

Where Herr Pfungst had blasted Kluge Hans as a fraud, subsequent critics found themselves frustrated by these amazing equine pupils of Krall, including the original Hans, for Pfungst's yardstick no longer applied. His contention had been based on his opinion that the horses themselves did nothing more than carry out the instructions or desires of the operator, orders which Pfungst held were transmitted, consciously or otherwise, by almost imperceptible changes of voice or position of the operator.

This theory came a cropper when applied to Hans and his new classmates under the tutelage of Herr Krall, for the horses could and did perform equally well regardless of whether their instructor was present. And to the great delight, if not edification, of the visiting scientists, the horses would sometimes interpose comments of their own in the midst of these sessions. Professor Clarapede reports that while he was conducting lengthy experiments at Elberfeld in the summer of 1913, Zarif suddenly stopped in the middle of the session.

The scientist wanted to know the reason for this.

'Tired,' Zarif tapped out. Then he added, 'Pain in leg.'

Drs. Schoeller and Gehrke state in their reports that during one of their numerous experiments with the Elderfeld horses (1912 and 1913) they asked Muhamed why he did not reply to them with speech instead of tapping out answers with his hoofs. The animal, they report, made pitiful and touching efforts to reproduce speech. After a few minutes of this, Muhamed went to his board and tapped out, 'I have not a good voice.'

Noting that he did not open his mouth when he tried to speak, they showed him by example that speech is possible only when the jaws are well separated. Then Dr. Gehrke asked, 'What must you do to speak?'

Replied Muhamed, 'Open mouth.'

'Why don't you open yours?'

'Because I can't.'

During some subsequent tests, Zarif was asked how he communicated with Muhamed.

'*Mit Mund.*' ('With mouth.')

'Why didn't you tell us that with your mouth, Zarif?'

'*Weil ich kein' Stimme habe.*' ('Because I have no voice.')

To the trio of Muhamed, Hans and Zarif was added the final member of Krall's famous stable, a blind stallion named Berto who compared favourably in his accomplishments with his colleagues. In 1912 Karl Krall published a book on the remarkable experiences which he and others had had with the horses of Elberfed. Their detractors were apparently confused by the fact that the horses did not require the presence of any particular person in order to do their mathematical problems, to reply to questions or to submit to such tests as scientists might contrive. If they felt like working they worked; if they did not feel like it, or if they disliked the visitors, they simply disregarded them.

Zoologists Kraemer and Ziegler of Stuttgart, Sarasin of Basle and many others supported Karl Krall's contention that he had proved Wilhelm Von Osten's theory regarding the latent mental abilities of animals, particularly of horses.

If his work proved nothing, it still served the purpose of refuting the criticism of Pfungst and of restoring the question to the realm of academic discussion.

In the December 17, 1914, issue of *Nature*, Dr. S. Von Maday wrote an article called 'Are There Talking Animals?' in which he said:

'. . . but the performance of the blind horse Berto stamps as inadequate Pfungst's theory of visually perceived movements. . . . The solution, if it ever comes, can scarcely fail to eliminate, if not the animal mind, at least that of man.'

The Strange Death of Napoleon

BONAPARTE, Napoleon: Born Corsica, 1769, died St. Helena, 1821.

At any rate, that's what the history books and encyclopedias say. But is it true?

Did Napoleon really die on the lonely isle of St. Helena? Why did the British government issue a conflicting report on his 'death'—a report which was belatedly admitted to be false in a major particular? And if Napoleon did not die as advertised—what happened to him, and how was it done?

It is a long, long story and in the beginning it originated with Napoleon, for it was he who took great pains to secure four doubles for himself many years before his empire began to collapse.

Of these doubles, painstakingly gathered by the Emperor's agents from all over Europe, one died of poisoning shortly before Waterloo and another was badly injured in a riding accident and left with a disability which made him useless as a stand-in for Napoleon.

Only two were left and one of them was François Eugene Robeaud, born in 1771 in the village of Baleycourt, in the Meuse. He bore such a remarkable resemblance to Napoleon in both face and figure that his fellow soldiers called him 'the Emperor'. It was routine and inevitable that this striking similarity should be brought to the great man's attention and Private Robeaud soon found himself living off the fat of the land, attached to Napoleon's personal staff.

After the Hundred Days, while Napoleon waited at Rochefort, his conquerors decided his fate. Of one thing the British wished to assure themselves: this time he must be exiled to a place from which escape would be impossible. There must not be another Elba, another Hundred Days.

To the sunbaked Isle of St. Helena he went, and according to the records of the British government, he died there of cancer after six years of confinement during which he was supposedly never left alone for a moment.

While the Eagle was chained to the rock off the coast of Africa, his double, François Robeaud, went back to Baleycourt to resume the life of a farmer. The French Minister of Police called in the special agent who had been assigned to watch Robeaud's movements. After all, the book was closed, and the bird was in the cage. Investigator Ledru was re-assigned to the less dramatic pursuit of tax-dodgers.

Napoleon had lost his freedom, but he still had many friends, and more important, his friends had plenty of money. His key to escape must be a golden key if it was to turn the lock that kept him in St. Helena. And it was a key that had to be carefully wrought, for there must be no slips. There could be but one attempt and it must not fail.

Now let us examine a very interesting series of apparently unrelated events in their chronological sequence:

In 1818 General Gourgard left his post of command at St. Helena and was replaced by General Bertrand. By a leisurely route, Gourgard made his way to Paris, where he lived quietly and unostentatiously. His contacts were chiefly with old friends from his years on the battlefields, old friends that included some very wealthy and influential persons who had ample funds and deep friendship for Napoleon.

About sixty days after Gourgard arrived in Paris, a fine coach drew up near the village of Baleycourt to inquire for a François

Robeaud. Neighbours directed the coach to Robeaud's humble cottage where he lived with his sister. Nobody recalled seeing the occupant or occupants of the coach, but passers-by later recalled that they had seen the coach itself standing beside the road a few rods from the lane that led to Robeaud's house. It was dark, however, and villagers who saw the conveyance went on about their business; they had learned through experience that they could not get into trouble by not asking questions.

Robeaud and his sister went about their routine duties for a month or so after the coach incident. The coach? Only a physician who wanted to buy some of Robeaud's rabbits as a gift for a friend. Nothing, really.

One morning in the autumn of 1818 a neighbour on his way to work noticed that the door of Robeaud's house was ajar. It was raining, and the wind was blowing the rain into the house. Strange, he thought, that François should be abed at this late hour —and with his door open, too! The neighbour went to close the door and glanced into the room. No fire on the hearth—now that was also very strange! Was something wrong with François and his sister? He called their names and received no reply.

Neither François Robeaud nor his sister were ever again seen in Baleycourt. They had left suddenly and in the night, taking few of their garments. Did they leave willingly?

The sister was seen in Paris two years later by two of the Baleycourt merchants, whom she pretended not to recognize. They notified the authorities and Inspector Ledru was again assigned to tracing down the elusive François Robeaud. This time Robeaud was not to be found, but Ledru did locate the sister living very comfortably in Tours. A physician explained that he had taken a fancy to her and was paying her bills. You understand, *n'est-ce-pas*? M. Ledru understood, up to a point, all right, but beyond that point he was left with a cranium full of question marks. This 'friendship' between the physician and the homely country girl from Baleycourt was not impossible (after all, there is no accounting for tastes!) but if it existed it must have been one of the most platonic friendships of its kind on record, for as nearly as Ledru and his men could determine, Robeaud's sister never even saw the wealthy physician who claimed to be so enamoured of her. Their arrangement was purely financial, and that by remote control—by courier, in fact.

Desperate at last, and worn out by weeks of pointless spying, the frustrated little inspector finally came out into the open.

'Where is your brother François?'

Miss Robeaud grinned. 'He is away on a trip. He decided to become a sailor and went away on a long voyage.'

What ship? She didn't know. When did he leave? Quite a while ago. When would he be back? She had no idea—François was always close-mouthed about such things, you see.

Poor M. Ledru finally gave up. The Robeaud house at Baley-court was shuttered and deserted. General Gourgard lived quietly in retirement. Robeaud's sister enjoyed fine living at someone else's expense in Tours. Napoleon's double was missing, but never mind—the government quietly checked with General Bertrand on St. Helena and was informed that the famous prisoner was still there. Of course. Where else would he be?

In order to escape from St. Helena, Napoleon needed three things—a ship, some friends and some money. With the last two, getting the first was easy.

Robeaud vanished from his native Baleycourt in the early autumn of 1818. By that time Napoleon had ceased to be of more than routine interest to the jittery British, and General Bertrand, who was certainly no hater of Napoleon, had been put in charge of the prisoner. It was in that year that General Bertrand's wife wrote to a friend: 'Success is ours! Napoleon has left the island!'

True or false?

In the closing days of 1818 a well-dressed stranger came to the city of Verona, Italy. He was, so he said, a merchant from the north of France. Now that his wife was dead and his children had homes of their own, he was fulfilling a lifetime desire to become a resident of Italy where he proposed to open a small shop or to buy one if the price was right and the requirements were light.

The shop he opened bore the sign of an optician, but, like most of its kind in those days, it dealt also in diamonds. The stranger, who called himself Revard, showed little interest in either optics or diamonds, preferring to let his partner, a Mr. Petrucci, handle the business. Revard bore a remarkable resemblance to Napoleon, as many people remarked, and his acquaintances called him 'The Emperor'—joking, of course. Petrucci often scolded him for giving away merchandise to impoverished couples who could not afford to buy what they wanted. Revard would only laugh and reimburse the till from his own ample purse.

On the afternoon of August 23, 1823, according to the subsequent testimony of Petrucci and others, a coach drew up in front of Revard's little shop and the coachman hurried inside. He handed Revard a letter which agitated the recipient greatly. Turning to Petrucci, he said: 'I find that I must leave at once on very important matters. I shall leave the shop in your hands. Please see that the coachman and the horses are properly cared for. I must retire to my room.'

About two hours late he came to Petrucci's house and handed him a thick letter written on parchment and sealed with wax in several places.

To his partner he said: 'I must leave on a long journey and these are evil times. If I am not back in three months, take this letter to the King of France. He will repay you for your services.'

Revard stepped into the waiting coach and it clattered away over the cobblestones.

Twelve nights later, on September 4, 1823, lights were blazing in Schönbrunn Castle in Austria, where the son of Napoleon was critically ill with scarlet fever. Shortly before eleven o'clock, one of the guards heard a rustling in the vines which spread over the high stone walls around the garden. A shadowy figure dropped to earth and ran towards the castle. The guard fired and the figure crumpled headlong.

The man was dead. His body was carried into a gardener's hut and authorities were called. They took one look and ordered the building locked and placed under guard. The next morning two high Austrian officials who had known Napoleon came to view the remains of the mysterious stranger who had been shot to death in the garden of Schönbrunn Castle. A few hours later representatives of the French Embassy came to claim the body But they did not keep it, for at the insistence of Napoleon's wife the body was returned to the castle and buried in an unmarked grave on a direct line with the spots which later held the remains of his wife and son.

'Revard' never returned to his shop in Verona.

Before Petrucci could deliver the letter to Paris, as instructed, a quartet of French officials arrived in Verona, liquidated the shop which had been operated by the mysterious 'M. Revard' and paid Signor Petrucci 100,000 gold crowns for the letter—and his silence. Petrucci maintained his silence on the subject for thirty years and then he told his story, under oath, to the authorities of Verona. He was confident, so he said, that his strange partner had been Napoleon Bonaparte.

Meanwhile, on sunbaked St. Helena, death came to the prisoner listed as Napoleon. Persons who knew the Emperor and who had visited him in his last days reported that exile had certainly wrought some remarkable changes in him. The 'Emperor' did not seem to be able to recall many of the incidents which should have been well known to him. He was rather rude and at times quite uncouth. The doctors who treated him showed little respect for their distinguished patient, if it was indeed Napoleon. Another unusual angle was added to the case when it came time to examine the will which the prisoner had left and which he had written about a year before his death. The handwriting shows numerous and marked differences from that of Napoleon, and eminent French authorities who examined the document expressed the opinion that 'Napoleon' had undergone some very pronounced changes 'brought on no doubt by his imprisonment'.

In the town records of Baleycourt there is inscribed the name of François Eugene Robeaud: 'born in this village, died on St. Helena. . . .' The date of Robeaud's alleged demise on St. Helena has been obliterated, perhaps for good reason, for in view of the existing evidence it is not impossible that he died there on May

5, 1821, under the name of Napoleon Bonaparte, whom he so closely resembled.

Still another tantalizing chapter is added to the circumstances surrounding Napoleon's death by the official British disclosure in the spring of 1956. After having closed the book on the Emperor in 1821 with the announcement that he had died of cancer of the stomach, the British waited one hundred and twenty-five years to reveal that they have a preserved section of Napoleon's intestine which is plainly perforated.

Oddly enough, the injury to the intestine corresponds closely to that which might have been made by a bayonet . . . or a bullet.

Was it the injury which caused Napoleon's death, as the British now assert?

Was it inflicted by a gunshot wound suffered in the garden of Schönbrunn Castle?

The answers to those questions would go far towards clearing up one of history's most celebrated mysteries—the true story of the death of Napoleon Bonaparte.

The Spark of Life

THE neighbours of Andrew Crosse regarded him as more devil than man. They did not understand the bright flashes that lighted his laboratory windows at nights when he tinkered with his crude electrical devices. Not only was he dreaded and shunned as 'the thunder and lightning man', but he was denounced as an atheist, a blasphemer and a Frankenstein, who had best be put in chains for the common safety.

Andrew Crosse minded his own business, it is true, but his was a very strange business for the first half of the nineteenth century. And one of his baffling experiences remains strange business to this day.

Having inherited a well-mortgaged and poorly kept estate in the Quantock Hills, Andrew settled down to the relatively humdrum routine of eking out a living, paying off his inherited debts and conducting himself in his spare time as an amateur scientist. In this latter endeavour he had little connection with others in the same field. Crosse laboured under the double handicap of not understanding his own experiments and not knowing about the accomplishments of others. This very lack of knowledge, perhaps, led him into the experience which has preserved his name.

Pottering around in his ramshackle laboratory, he decided to conduct some experiments on the formation and development of artificial crystals by means of prolonged exposure to weak electric currents. He rigged up a small chunk of porous stone (oxide of iron from Mt. Vesuvius) and kept it electrified by means of a crude battery. Dunking this arrangement in a solution of hydrochloric acid and silicate of potash, Crosse hoped to create some artificial crystals of silica. He attached the wires to the lump of iron oxide and set the equipment on a small table where it would be out of the way while he went back to his regular pastime of studying the spark-gap—the flashes which alarmed his neighbours.

Did he accidentally hit upon an arrangement which created life out of inorganic matter?

In a paper which he wrote for the London Electrical Society in that same year of 1837 Andrew Crosse set down this account of his experience:

'On the fourteenth day from the commencement of this experiment I observed through a small lens a few small whitish excrescences or nipples, projecting from about the middle of the electrified stone. On the eighteenth day these projections enlarged and struck out seven or eight filaments, each of them longer than the hemisphere on which they grew.

On the twenty-sixth day these appearances assumed the form of a *perfect insect* standing erect on a few bristles which formed its tail. Till this period I had no notion that these appearances were other than an incipient mineral formation. On the twenty-eighth day these little creatures moved their legs. I must say now that I was not a little astonished. After a few days they detached themselves from the stone and moved about at pleasure.

In the course of a few weeks, about a hundred of them made their appearance on the stone. I examined them with a microscope and observed that the smaller ones appeared to have only six legs; the larger ones had eight. These insects are pronounced to be of the genus *acarus*, but there appears to be a difference of opinion whether they are a known species; some assert that they are not.

I have never ventured an opinion on the cause of their

birth, and for a very good reason—I was unable to form one. The simplest solution of the problem which occurred to me was that they arose from ova deposited by insects floating in the atmosphere and hatched by electric action. Still I could not imagine that an ovum could shoot out filaments, or that these filaments should become bristles, and moreover I could not detect, on the closest examination, the remains of a shell. I next imagined, as others have done, that they might originate in the water and consequently made a close examination of numbers of vessels filled with the same fluid: in none of these could I perceive a trace of an insect, nor could I see any in any other part of the room.'

The puzzled amateur scientist was well aware of the tightrope he was walking. He was describing an experience which did not fit into the accepted pattern of science; therefore he was inviting ridicule, if not worse. Crosse had to be careful.

He suspected that the myserious 'insects' might be stowaways on his porous stone, so he dispensed with the stone entirely and conducted experiments with glass jars filled only with various acids—copper nitrate, copper sulphate and zinc sulphate. Again and again his little visitors appeared in the solutions. He found, so he wrote, that these *acari* appeared first beneath the surface of the acid, but after once emerging from their acid birthplace, they quickly died if dropped back into it.

'Fraud!' cried his detractors. Learned men denounced both Crosse and his 'insects' as nothing more than humbugs, the product of airborne spores or of impurities in the fluids themselves.

Crosse had anticipated the critics there. He had already begun a new series of experiments designed to determine whether or not the things he saw were the result of electrical generation and nothing more. Crosse boiled his jars. He baked some of the apparatus in an oven. He filled the receivers over inverted mercury troughs with manufactured oxygen and super-heated his silicate solutions. Crosse took these precautions to ensure the sterility of the materials used. Yet, on the one-hundred-and-fortieth day after he sent the current into his sealed, air-free jars, the mysterious *acari* appeared as before. Cross discovered one of the creatures shortly before it slipped from the side of the bulb and fell back into the caustic solution where it quickly died. He blamed himself for not remembering that once they had left the acid they could not return to it and live. Moreover, he had provided no place for them to survive.

In an atmosphere strongly impregnated with deadly chlorine, he produced still more of the creatures—fully developed, he says, but devoid of life. They floated about in the lethal liquid for two years until he finally dismantled the equipment.

Other scientists conducted similar experiments—with similar results. There was, however, one noteworthy oddity in connection with their findings: when they used sterile equipment and allowed electric current to flow through the fluids, the mysterious 'insects' always appeared. The weaker the current, the longer was the period required for the appearance of the so-called *acari*. They also found that with identical solutions, and the current omitted, there would be no *acari* development. By increasing the proportion of carbon in the fluids, the number of 'insects' was increased in somewhat similar proportion.

Of course there was a furore in the scientific circles of his time over the mystifying developments reported from the laboratory of Andrew Crosse. Standing virtually alone and unknown against the tide of calumny, he could only repeat doggedly that he had told the truth, as some of his detractors could readily determine if they would conduct similar experiments. Suddenly the assault upon him died down, for he found a champion whom the critics dared not question. The great Michael Faraday reported to the Royal Institution that he, too, had experienced the development of these little creatures in the course of his experiments. Faraday could not decide whether to regard them as having been created in the solutions or as having been brought back to life by the actions of the current!

Crosse made no claims of having created anything, unusual or otherwise. He merely tried to report to his contemporaries what he had seen and the conditions under which these things had transpired. Patiently he noted the striking similarity between the lifeless mineral crystals and the *acari*, how each first appeared in the acid solutions as minute white specks. He wrote:

'Each mineral speck enlarges and elongates vertically: so it does with the *acarus*. Then the mineral throws out whitish filaments: so does the *acarus* speck. So far it is difficult to detect the difference between the incipient mineral and the animal; but as these filaments become more definite in each, in the mineral they become rigid, shining and transparent six-sided prisms; in the animal, they become soft and waving filaments and finally are endowed with life and motion.'

Andrew Crosse lived many years after his remarkable announcement of 1837. He was a happy man, pottering away in his laboratory at Quantock, seeking truth and living as he pleased, until Death came for him on July 6, 1855, in the same room in which he had been born.

Although he spent his life in the quest for scientific truths, the sole contribution for which Andrew Crosse is remembered is the controversy over his '*acari*'—unwanted then and unsolved today.

The Vanishing Village

In the annals of the Royal Canadian Mounted Police is the strange story of an entire village that disappeared. It was a case where the Mounties not only did not find their man; neither did they find the women and children.

For many years a tribe of Eskimos had been making camp for the winter at Lake Angikuni, about five hundred miles northwest of the Mountie base at Churchill. It was a convenient spot for them, near enough to hunting grounds for them to survive, and still far enough from civilization that they could live as they pleased. This very isolation may also have played a part in their strange fate, whatever it was.

Occasional nomadic trappers visited the Eskimos at this lonely spot, swapped talk, ate caribou, smoked a few pipes of trade tobacco and swapped furs. Such a visitor was a French-Canadian named Joe LaBelle. He knew the country and the people like he knew the back of his hand, having roamed that part of the wilderness for more than forty years. In November of 1930 Joe was on his way back to civilization from a moderately successful trapping and trading trip and he changed his course slightly so that he could spend a few days with his friends at the lonely outpost on Lake Angikuni.

The first intimation that something was amiss came as he started down the slight slope that led to the village. Instead of the customary uproar from the community's dogs, he was greeted by silence.

According to Joe's report to the Mounted Police, he stopped at the edge of the little village and shouted a greeting. No reply of any kind. He thought it exceedingly strange, he said, for these were friendly folk who were always glad to see visitors, especially such old friends as Joe LaBelle.

He opened the caribou-skin flap that served as a door to one of the low sod huts and called again. Silence. A similar experience awaited him at the next tent.

Very, very spooky, said Mr. LaBelle to himself, for there was no one else to say it to.

LaBelle subsequently reported to the Mounted Police that he spent about an hour in the deserted village, examining the score of tents and huts for some clue to the strange disappearance of the residents. He found pots of food hanging over cooking fires which had been cold for weeks, perhaps for months. In one hut were some sealskin garments for a child. The ivory needle was still sticking in the garment where the mother had abruptly ceased her mending. On the beach were three kayaks, including one which he knew had belonged to the headman. These flimsy craft were battered by wave action on the beach, evidence that they had been neglected for a considerable period of time.

But the most puzzling bits of evidence were back in the village.

There, LaBelle (and the Mounted Police who came afterwards) found the Eskimos' prized rifles standing forlornly, waiting for masters who never returned. Now a rifle is more than a prized possession to these simple folk—it is a life insurance policy. No Eskimo in his right mind would start on an extended trip without his rifle, yet here were the guns—and the Eskimos were gone.

What about the dogs?

About a hundred yards from the deserted camp, LaBelle found seven dogs. They had been tied to the stumps of some scrub trees. All had been dead for some time, and it was Joe's guess from their appearance that they had died of starvation, which was later

C

confirmed by the examination of Canadian government pathologists.

On the other side of the camp from the spot where the dogs were found LaBelle came upon still another baffling phase of this case. There the Eskimos had buried some member of their tribe with the customary covering of stones over the grave. But this grave had been opened and the body removed—a procedure that would be unthinkable to Eskimos. The grave-rifling had been done by someone who had carefully stacked the covering stones in two neat piles. It could not have been the work of animals—and whoever did it left no clues.

LaBelle made haste to Churchill, where he repeated his eerie experience to the Mounted Police. He accompanied them back to the deserted village, where they found things just as he had described them. For reasons unknown, a village of about thirty inhabitants had been deserted in the dead of winter, and for reasons unknown the Eskimos had abandoned the place so hurriedly that they had left their clothing, food and guns behind—and had left their dogs to starve. And the rifled grave? Just another bit of unexplained mystery.

Months of investigation among other tribes in the area brought no trace of any member of the band which had lived in the village on Angikuni. The Mounted Police finally filed it away as an unsolved mystery, and so it remains.

Who Shot Abraham Lincoln?

Who shot Abraham Lincoln?

A screwball actor who called himself J. Wilkes Booth?

What happened to Mr. Booth?

He was shot to death, so we are told, by a religious fanatic identified as Sergeant Boston Corbett.

Who were the conspirators who carried out this dastardly deed? Why did they do it? Were they all brought to justice? If not, why not?

Let's look at the record.

A pistol-shot that rang out in the semi-gloom of Ford's Theatre on the night of April 14, 1865, started more rumours and resulted in more misinformation than any similar interval of time in America's history.

The basic facts are quickly arrived at: Scores of people heard the pop of the little derringer that fired the fatal shot and saw the President slump in his chair. Hundreds of people saw a man leap from the President's box to the stage, stumble and fall—then, mumbling a few words and brandishing a knife, the man limped across the stage and vanished.

There fact ends and fantasy begins, for in spite of months of questioning that was conducted with all the calm and logic of a bar-room brawl, in spite of millions of words of testimony both factual and false, the most appalling crime in American annals is still studded with question marks, many of them contributed by the actions of Mr. Lincoln's own Secretary of War, fierce, turbulent, power-loving Edwin M. Stanton. The role that Mr. Stanton played is indeed strangest of all.

Let's turn back the calendar to the known facts of April, 1865, and start from there.

The war had just ended. The nation was prostrate, suffering from inflation, dissension and national fatigue in all its forms. Lincoln's Cabinet was sharply divided as to what moves to make. The radical wing of the Republican party, led by Vice-President Andrew Johnson, was determined to see that never again should the South be anything except the puppet of the industrialized North. Lincoln opposed this viewpoint. He wanted to restore the South to its place in the sun.

Andrew Johnson wanted to be President, and he made no bones about it. That could happen only if Lincoln died, for Johnson had probably ended his own political chances by appearing drunk to take the oath of office at Lincoln's second inauguration.

Fate had set the stage for tragedy.

That pistol-shot in the shadows of Ford's Theatre brought Andrew Johnson to the presidency, which he could probably never have attained otherwise. Another shot, in Garret's barn near Fredricksburg, Virginia, a few days later, sealed the lips of a man who might have explained the first shot.

About a month before the assassination of Lincoln, a War Department employee named Louis Weichmann told his co-workers that plotters were meeting at Mary Surratt's boarding house, concocting schemes against the President's life. Since Weichmann lived there himself, there was reason to credit his story, but somehow it got lost in the numerous alarms and rumours of plots which were current. Weichmann was an employee of the agency headed by Mr. Stanton, but if Weichmann's alarming story ever reached Stanton there is no record of it, and certainly no action was taken to question the man who claimed to be in possession of such dangerous knowledge. Weichmann continued to board at Surratt's and the plotters continued to conspire, unmolested by even a routine check.

Lafayette C. Baker, head of the Secret Service, boasted that he had two thousand informers in Washington. Yet if Baker knew of the witch's cauldron to which Weichmann referred, there is no evidence of it from Baker or his superior, Mr. Stanton. Under the circumstances, it would seem very strange indeed if neither Stanton nor Baker heard of Weichmann's story, and stranger still if they heard of it and made no attempt to investigate.

They made a good team, this Lafayette Baker and Edwin Stanton. Stanton was a clever attorney, at times a brilliant barrister. He was crafty, too, and not above lying when it served his ends. Hard, cruel and highly emotional, he found in Lafayette Baker an ideal tool for carrying out some of his designs.

The head of the Secret Service was merely shifty where Stanton was smart. Baker had few scruples which would prevent him from attaining his ends. Disliked by Lincoln, he found in Stanton a superior who gave him the support he needed to conduct some very questionable operations.

They worked together through the war itself and now, in these darkened hours of April 14, 1865, they were still working together, but not as closely as during the war years. Perhaps their coolness was a result of a growing mutual distrust. For whatever reason, Stanton sent Baker to New York City. And when the greatest case of his career broke, Baker found himself 250 miles away by orders of the Secretary of War.

Contrary to popular belief, Mr. Stanton did not urge General Grant to stay away from Ford's Theatre that fateful night. General Grant arrived at that decision himself, knowing that Mrs. Lincoln and Mrs. Grant did not enjoy each other's company. The General attended a Cabinet meeting in mid-afternoon and when it had been concluded he thanked the President for the theatre invitation and regretted that he could not attend, since he had promised Mrs. Grant that they would leave that night to visit their two children in New Jersey.

When President Lincoln came to Mr. Stanton's office that same afternoon, Mr. Lincoln said that he was looking for someone to go with him to the theatre that night and he asked Stanton if he might take Major Thomas Eckert, head of the telegraph office—a powerfully built fellow whose strength was well known to the President.

Stanton refused the President's request on the ground that Major Eckert had some very important work which must be done that night. Yet when Stanton closed his office for the day he made no mention of any special duties for Major Eckert, another puzzling aspect of Stanton's performance which was never explained.

While Mr. Lincoln kept his appointment with destiny that night, Mr. Stanton paid a visit to the home of Secretary Seward, who was then convalescing from injuries suffered in a carriage accident. Stanton left Seward's home about nine o'clock, which was already past Stanton's regular bedtime, and when the first news of Lincoln's assassination was brought to him, about ten o'clock, Stanton was still not in bed, but, according to some witnesses, was nervously pacing the floor. He was certainly not in bed when the news came, for his wife later stated that after being notified that the President had been shot, Mr. Stanton went upstairs, undressed, and went to bed!

A few minutes later, when more couriers came to inform him of what he already knew, Stanton scrambled into his clothes and into a waiting carriage which took him to the house where the President was dying.

For a man of Stanton's mental stature, his subsequent actions are difficult to analyse. Those who suspect him of a guilty conscience can explain his vagaries easily enough. But if we are to give him the benefit of every doubt we find ourselves confronted with the spectacle of a brilliant, dynamic individual who suddenly steps out of character and performs like a man in a complete state of funk.

When the assassin leapt from the President's box to the stage of the theatre, many persons who knew John Wilkes Booth saw and recognized him. This fact was reported to Stanton when the Secretary arrived at the scene of the crime about an hour after the shooting. But instead of spreading the alarm and identifying the killer as quickly as possible, Stanton lost precious time by setting up a court of inquiry in a back room of the Peterson house, where the stricken President lay gasping. While Booth was slipping away in the night, Stanton was playing judge.

The records show that Booth rode out of Washington without difficulty, because he crossed the Potomac at the Navy Yard Bridge, the only bridge which was not closed. For years it had been closed every night at nine o'clock. But on this night of all nights Booth had no difficulty in crossing it at ten-thirty. Coincidence perhaps? If that is what it was, then it was of a part with the fact that the order for troops to patrol the roads and scour the countryside around Washington neglected to include the roads of southern Maryland, which Booth was using on his escape route.

In a room of the Peterson house, Edwin M. Stanton had set himself up as the acting head of government. From that point he was taking testimony, snapping orders to military and civil officials, directing the search for the assassin.

One hour and thirty minutes after the shooting of Mr. Lincoln, Stanton sent out his first order to apprehend the person or persons who had shot the President. The identity of the man they wanted was a matter of common knowledge by this time, yet Stanton does not even mention Booth's name in his order. Nor had any effort been made to locate and search Booth's room.

Shortly after twelve-thirty on the morning of April 15th, Stanton held a hurried conference with half a dozen police and military officials. At that time the bristling little Secretary of War disclosed that the assassin was John Wilkes Booth, but then he warned them that he wanted no public announcement of this fact yet. Why? Stanton never explained that action. It becomes another question mark in Mr. Stanton's role on this memorable occasion.

Stanton's wire to General Grant was delivered to the General at Baltimore. Grant noted at the end of the telegram that special arrangements were being made to rush him back to Washington. Then he tucked the telegram in his pocket and went on to Burlington, New Jersey, to visit his children.

Other telegrams were on their way from Stanton by this time, one of them to the Chief of the New York Police Department asking him to send some reliable detectives. But there was no telegram to the Chief of the Secret Service, Lafayette Baker, the government's own top investigator.

John Wilkes Booth had five precious hours in which to make his way unmolested towards freedom. But for the mishap which broke a small bone in his leg, he might have made it.

Three hours after Stanton took control of the situation the authorities knew the identities of four men who were involved in the plot: Booth, Herold, Paine and Atzerodt. Still no mention of any of them in the official bulletins that went out from Stanton's office. Newpapermen were pressing for some quotable mention of Booth's participation in the crime, but Stanton maintained his silence. The first Press release was handed out at a few minutes past two o'clock on the morning of the 15th—and it contained no reference to Booth. Editors of morning papers had to go to press shortly, minus the official confirmation of the name that would live in infamy.

Another hour dragged by. The tall, gaunt man in the back bedroom at the Peterson house was slowly slipping away. Andrew Johnson had come to spend a few minutes beside Lincoln's bed and had gone back to his room to await the call that could come at any moment.

Five hours after the actual shooting, Stanton finally named the culprit in a telegram to Major-General John A. Dix in New York City.

Investigation strongly indicates J. Wilkes Booth as the assassin of the President, said Stanton's message, and he added: *Every exertion has been made to prevent the escape of the murderer*.

Shortly before daylight, the Secretary of War belatedly agreed to permit the distribution of pictures of the assassin in order to facilitate his capture. Instead of clarifying matters, this action merely added another element of mystery to the strange events of that fateful night, for the picture which Stanton approved and sent out was not that of John Wilkes Booth, but of his brother, the famous Edwin Booth!

Although the President had been shot shortly after ten o'clock on the night of April 14th, Stanton did not notify the head of the Secret Service until noon of the following day. He wired Baker in New York City: *Come here immediately and see if you can find the murderer of the President.* Baker took the next train and stepped into the maddest moments of his career.

By the time he reached Washington, Booth had been gone for thirty-six hours. Confusion was rampant. Lincoln was dead; Johnson had become President; Stanton's self-assigned role of Acting President was being whittled down. To make matters worse, the Army (which was under Stanton's direction) was flatly refusing to co-operate with the police or the Secret Service. Secretary of State Seward issued orders that the assassin was to be brought back alive—but Stanton refused to pass the order along to the troops which were searching for Booth.

This was the situation into which Baker was suddenly projected. Being an accomplished conniver himself, he may have smelled a rat. At any rate he wasted no time getting to Stanton and the two of them held a conference that lasted for hours.

There was something less than complete accord between Stanton and the head of the Secret Service. For instance, Stanton knew that Booth had broken his leg, but Baker was not told. Stanton also knew that the Army was keeping one of the conspirators under lock and key, but Baker didn't find that out, either.

He spent most of his time behind his desk, wrangling with the Army, bluffing with the newsmen and waiting for something. He published some pictures of certain persons wanted for questioning, including Booth. Newspapers had already detected the error in the Booth pictures released by Stanton and had switched to pictures of the killer. Baker acted as a buffer for Stanton, keeping the Secretary of War out of the limelight for the time being at least.

Lafayette Baker was simply waiting. He wasted little time on the flood of tips that poured in from all parts of the nation where Booth was supposedly seen. Baker got what he was waiting for.

His cousin, Lieutenant Luther Baker, came in around noon on Monday, April 24th, and was taken immediately into a private conference with the head of the Secret Service. A few minutes later, Lafayette Baker hurried over to Stanton's office. Then, with twenty-five armed men, he rode down to the boat that took the party to the Maryland peninsula. In the presence of witnesses the head of the Secret Service said: 'You boys have a sure thing. You are going after Booth.'

Secretary of State Seward had repeated his demands that the killer of Mr. Lincoln be brought in alive. Stanton had not passed that order on to Baker, although other searching parties had finally been advised. And it was Baker who gave instructions to the men who were sent out to apprehend the killer. On the witness stand later, Lieutenant Baker said that Stanton had told him exactly where he would find the man he sought but had issued no instructions to bring him in alive. Had he been instructed to kill the fugitive? Somehow that question was not put to the witness.

What actually happened when the troops surrounded the barn where their quarry was concealed?

Testimony and military records show that the troops found two men in the barn to which they had been directed. When the men refused to come out, the troops set fire to the structure. One man, David Herold, came stumbling out, whining for mercy, chattering that he had 'always liked Mr. Lincoln's jokes'. A trooper kicked him and told him to shut up; other soldiers tied him to a tree.

Inside the barn a man on crutches was hobbling around, plainly visible in the light from the blazing straw. He shifted his carbine to his left hand, drew his revolver with his right and said: 'Well, boys, you can prepare a stretcher for me. One more stain on the old banner!' With that there was the sound of a shot and the man inside the barn stiffened and fell headlong.

A crackpot trooper, Boston Corbett, immediately claimed that he had shot the fugitive to death. The evidence indicates otherwise. The wound was in the back of the neck and was a pistol wound at that, fired from such short range that Booth had been powder-burned. Corbett had been thirty feet away when the shot was fired. The man who ran into the barn just as the shot rang out was Lieutenant Luther Baker.

In death as in life, John Wilkes Booth was a subject of violent controversy. There were those who denied that the man who was shot to death in that barn near Fredricksburg was really Booth. They based their argument primarily on the testimony of Doctor John Mays, who testified that when he was called to identify the remains, he had done so reluctantly because, he said, 'There was no resemblance to Booth and I do not believe it was Booth!'

The doctor was wrong.

Lafayette Baker wrapped the body in canvas, rowed it through heavy fog to the monitor *Montauk* which was waiting out in the river. At Stanton's orders a burial party had been sworn to secrecy and the body of Booth was buried under the floor of an old prison in Washington, in a room to which only Stanton had a key. Many years later the government relented and permitted the family to identify the body and to take it for final interment in an unmarked grave.

The man who was silenced forever by a pistol-shot in that barn was the man who had shot to death Abraham Lincoln.

Lafayette Baker says that when he went to Secretary Stanton's office to break the news of Booth's death, he first told Stanton that Booth had been found. Then, says Baker, Stanton dropped onto a couch and covered his face with his hands without saying a word. When he was told that Booth was dead, Stanton removed his hands from his face and smiled for the first time in days—according to Baker.

The diary that was found on Booth's body was turned over to the head of the Secret Service, who testified that he in turn delivered it to Mr. Stanton. At the time he gave it to Stanton the diary was complete up to April 25th, immediately prior to Booth's death. Stanton first denied having the diary but later reversed himself and brought it into court. More than two dozen pages covering the period of the conspiracy leading up to Lincoln's death were missing. Baker told the court that the diary had been complete when he had turned it over to Stanton. At Stanton's request the court officially ruled that no deletions had been made from the diary.

The assassin died from a pistol wound inflicted by a party who was never officially identified. Mary Surratt, George Atzerodt, Lewis Payne and David Herold were all hanged one blazing July day. The public clamour for blood had been appeased. Justice had been done, and the guilty had paid for their crime.

At least that was the general understanding.

There remained a few loose ends which were left dangling.

For some unknown reason, there was no investigation to clear up the strange fact that the assassination of Abraham Lincoln was reported in at least two newspapers several hours before it happened! In St. Joseph, Minnesota, and in Middletown, New York, newspapers featured the assassination stories 'from reliable sources' while the President was still alive, on the afternoon of that fateful Good Friday. In view of the subsequent events which supported those premature reports, it is strange indeed that the ubiquitous Mr. Stanton, with his characteristic attention to detail, made no effort to trace the source of such prophetic reporting.

It is also a matter of record that the two principal witnesses for the State in the conspiracy trial were Louis Weichmann and John Lloyd. Weichmann was the War Department employee who boarded at Mrs. Surratt's and who spread the story of the plot that was being hatched there, a story which was officially ignored, at least prior to the actual crime.

John Lloyd was a minor figure who suddenly assumed damning proportions. He was a drunken tavern-keeper who was admittedly deep in his cups at the time Mrs. Surratt allegedly came to deliver to him a pair of field glasses and to remind him to have the guns ready—'Parties will call for them tonight.' In spite of his admittedly bad condition (falling-down drunkenness), at the trial John Lloyd's ability to remember every word with startling clarity helped put the nooses around the necks of Mrs. Surratt and her co-conspirators.

But after the trial was over and after Stanton had finally been forced out of office by President Johnson, Lloyd and Weichmann found courage to complain in public.

Lloyd maintained that he had been threatened with death or long imprisonment if he refused to testify as he had done. Perhaps he was just trying to excuse himself; perhaps he was telling the truth. At any rate that was one story that he never changed.

Louis Weichmann left the War Department for a job with the Post Office. It was, he said, his reward for being such a co-operative witness in the trial of the conspirators, a reward promised to him by Secretary Edwin M. Stanton. Weichmann became a progressively poorer employee, a man who seemed to feel that he could do pretty much as he pleased, since Stanton was backing him. He got the surprise of his life one morning when he was summarily dismissed from the government service. Weichmann railed and ranted, but in vain. Mr. Stanton could no longer help him; he, too, was having troubles.

The actual shooting of Mr. Lincoln was made possible by the absence of the guard who was detailed to the door of the President's box in Ford's Theatre. John Booth was there, John Parker was not.

A precious character, this John F. Parker. He became a member of the Washington police force in 1861 after a ninety-day bit in the Army. By the fall of '62 Parker was already embroiled with his superiors for insubordination, for which he was reprimanded. A few months later he was charged with sleeping on duty, firing his pistol without provocation through the window of a bawdy house (where he was residing for a few weeks!), and for cursing a lady on the street while drunk on duty.

This was John F. Parker, who became a guard for the President by specific orders of Mrs. Lincoln on April 3, 1863. How or why she ever endorsed such a dissolute person for such a task is one of the unexplained mysteries of the Lincoln tragedy. If Parker had been planted on the White House staff by Lafayette Baker, the Secret Service chief, it would have been quite in keeping with the character of the man. Baker claimed to have access to the White House at all times and he was of considerable service to himself and to his superior, Mr. Stanton, by keeping informed on what went on inside the Executive Mansion. Since Mr. Lincoln openly distrusted and detested Baker, it is quite possible that Baker's claims of being the confidant of Mrs. Lincoln had an element of truth in them. In this fashion, perhaps, John F. Parker, the outcast city policeman, became a member of the White House staff in April of '63 and became a factor in the murder of the President in April of 1865.

The guard for the President was the key man in the plans of the conspirators, for unless that guard could be eliminated, any commotion, shouting or scuffling with the guard would alert those inside the box with the President as well as those nearby in the theatre itself. The ideal situation from the murderer's standpoint would be a guard who left his post. Parker obligingly did just that.

Instead of remaining at his station to protect the unsuspecting President, Parker ran true to form and went next door to slake his interminable thirst at Taltuval's saloon. He was there drinking when Booth came in and saw him. Parker remained at the bar. Booth left. When John Wilkes Booth saw the President's body-guard in that saloon he knew that the way to murdering the President was clear. Was it mere coincidence that these two men happened to meet at that time at that place?

Parker's confused actions for the balance of that terrible night are both unusual and unimportant. He had deserted his post and forfeited the life of a beloved President. The fact that Parker stumbled around in the rain all night and finally dragged a poor old drunken prostitute into a police station early next morning is not important. But the fact that John F. Parker was never prosecuted for his failure to protect the President *is* important. Yet the *record shows* that no charges were ever filed against him and he actually remained a member of the police force for three more years! In other words, Parker left the police force just about the time that Stanton was forced out of the Cabinet. Coincidence? Perhaps.

Officially, the assassination of Lincoln was solved with the death of Booth and the execution of four of his co-conspirators. Left unanswered were many facets of the case: Why was Booth able to find and use the only bridge that was open that night? Why was that bridge still open? Why were troops not sent to search the roads of southern Maryland, the only area they did not search that night and the only area that Booth could (and did) use? Why did Stanton withhold Booth's name from the public until five hours after the shooting? Why did Stanton release the picture of Edwin Booth as that of the killer, when they bore little facial resemblance? Why did Stanton wait until fourteen hours after the shooting to call Lafayette Baker back to Washington? Why were Seward's orders to take the assassin alive not passed on by Stanton until he was forced to take that action? Did the party of soldiers sent to get Booth have orders to take him alive? Who really fired the shot that killed Booth? What happened to the pages which Baker claimed were missing from Booth's diary? Why did Stanton first deny that he had the diary? Why was John Parker never even fired for deserting his post?

The assassination of Abraham Lincoln is indeed a strange story in which the unexplained actions of Edwin M. Stanton are the strangest of all.

Desert Dreadnought

I⊤ was indeed a strange name for a battleship, but then the *Arakwe* was a strange battleship. In all the annals of the American Navy there was never another ship that came to such an unusual end, for the *Arakwe* fought her one and only battle on dry land!

She was a side-wheeler, a wooden ship with huge paddle-wheels in covered boxes on the sides of the vessel, just like the handful of river boats which still ply the inland streams for dances and excursions. The *Arakwe* was proud but *passé*. Built in the closing days of the Civil War, she got her commission too late for action in that conflict. And perhaps it is just as well, for wooden vessels had already been outmoded by the ironclads. She was fitted up with a couple of small cannon, given a captain and a crew, and listed as a gunboat.

The *Arakwe* bummed around the Caribbean for a couple of years before she drifted down the coast and around the Horn to Aconaqua in Chile. Her orders were to act as a morale-builder for the shaky Chilean government just by sticking around and showing her two small guns and waving the Stars and Stripes at her masthead.

This sort of thing went on for more than a year. Captain Alexander and his crew were getting restless. The sturdy craft needed some repairs and the skipper asked for permission to return to the States. Permission was granted, but it came too late.

The steam launch had brought the mail from shore and

Captain Alexander was sitting in his cabin reading the communications which were at least a month old. He found the one he wanted ordering him to take the *Arakwe* to Pensacola. Ah! Pensacola! That meant at least a month of welcome relief from the dreary duties that had plagued him for the past year.

The Captain's log picks up the story at that point:

'While servicing the mail which had just arrived I noticed that the cabin lamp was swinging fore and aft. This I thought most unusual since we were anchored well inside the bay and there was no wind. I hurried on deck and quickly recognized the nature of the disturbance as a submarine earthquake, since the water was rapidly draining seaward from the bay. By prompt action we managed to swing the *Arakwe* around, but in a matter of minutes we were aground, our stern to the sea.

I anticipated that we might be able to ride it out by cutting the anchor cable which was quickly accomplished. The stench from the sun shining on the mud of the harbour bottom was most distressing and several of the crew were made ill. Others, including the officers, managed to avoid this condition by breathing only through clean cloths soaked in vinegar, a practice to be recommended in such circumstances.

The great wave which struck us broke over the stern of the ship and did heavy damage as well as sweeping overboard three members of the crew who were never seen again. We had no control of the ship and indeed counted ourselves fortunate to be afloat.'

Riding the wildly churning waters of the tidal wave, the old *Arakwe* was flung inland along with scores of other craft. Thanks to her shallow draft and flat-bottomed construction, she rode it like a raft, coming to rest at the foot of a cliff two miles from the sea. All about her was scattered the wreckage of other vessels and their cargoes. The deep sand along the base of the cliff was strewn for miles with tempting bait for looters.

D

The looters came to prey on the plunder. Alexander armed his crew with pistols and warned the swarms of looters away. When morning came he realized that he was in for real trouble. Most of the worthwhile items had already been carried away from the desert strip where the sea had deposited the wreckage, and during the night the number of voracious plunderers had multiplied. Many of them tried to climb aboard the *Arakwe*; the tired crew beat them off with difficulty. The looters crowded together just out of pistol range: the *Arakwe's* hour was at hand.

Captain Alexander ordered the cannon loaded. The gun crew managed to get enough powder, but they were unable to reach the shot, which was somewhere in the twisted wreckage beneath the sloping deck. In desperation the Captain bethought himself of a substitute—hard round cheeses from the galley.

The mob surged over the sand towards the old battleship, screaming and firing pistols. Alexander held his fire until they were only a couple of hundreds yards away. Then the cannon roared—and balls of cheese skipped over the sand. A couple of men were bowled over like ninepins, only to leap to their feet and scurry out of danger. Another broadside did the job; the mob retreated in wild disorder, surfeited with cheese.

The *Arakwe* never got back to the sea. She was broken up where she lay, sprawled in the sand miles from the water. In the Navy's records she is gallantly listed as lost in action, which in a sense she was. But the *Arakwe* is more than that, for she is the battleship that fought her only battle on dry land, firing cheese at a gang of thieves.

The Restless Dead

To all appearances it was going to be just another routine funeral ceremony, but Fate had prepared a surprise for those who attended the interment of the Honourable Thomas Chase on that hot summer day in 1812.

The deceased had held several minor government positions on Barbados; he had dabbled in some small shipping ventures and in trade with the Yankees. The Honourable Thomas Chase was not wealthy but was quite well-to-do, enough so that several prominent officials of the island of Barbados attended final services for him.

In the yard of Christ Church, overlooking Oistin's Bay, Barbados, the Chase family had built a heavy stone vault, partially underground, to receive the bodies of their dead. It was to this place that the funeral cortège of the Honourable T. Chase made its way after services had been conducted in the nearby church by the Reverend Thomas H. Orderson. This was to be the fourth burial in the family vault; Mrs. Thomasina Goddard had been buried there on July 31, 1807; Mary Ann Chase, infant daughter of the Honourable Thomas Chase, was buried there on February 22, 1808; Dorcas Chase, another daughter, was interred in the same vault on July 6, 1812.

Those three burials gave no hint of anything unusual about the vault in which the bodies were placed, so the funeral party was utterly unprepared for what happened when they pried up

51

the heavy stone slab that sealed the tomb on August 9, 1812, in order to put the body of Thomas Chase in its last resting place.

According to the account of the Reverend Orderson who was present at the time, the negroes who lifted the slab refused to carry Mr. Chase's body down the five steps that led to the vault. They appeared to be greatly agitated, says Reverend Orderson, and were most adamant in their refusal to proceed further with the task at hand.

Small wonder! When Orderson and others of the burial party peered into the vault they found the coffins of Mary Ann Chase and Dorcas Chase out of the places in which they had been seen only a few days before at the burial of Dorcas. The coffin of little Mary Ann was on the other side of the vault, about six feet from where it had originally been placed, and was standing head down against the wall.

After the initial confusion had subsided, those in charge of burying the Honourable Thomas Chase proceeded with their assignment, first replacing the coffins of the three prior occupants and then carefully lowering that of Mr. Chase to a spot on the floor of the vault. It was no easy task, for we are told that he was a big man, and he was encased in a lead shell over an inner cedar box. Small wonder that it required the exertions of eight husky men to handle it.

The Barbados authorities were considerably disturbed about the incident. Had someone violated the grave in an attempt to rob the bodies? The church board met with the civil officials and the workmen at the cemetery were given an intensive grilling. It was fruitless, for in reality there was nothing to support the attempted robbery theory. The coffins had been moved but there was no sign that any effort had been made to open them. With a sharp reprimand from the frustrated investigators, the workmen were sent back to their jobs. Guards were posted around the cemetery and required to inspect the seals on the Chase vault twice each day. Nothing unusual occurred at that vault or any other.

Four years after the disturbing discovery at the funeral of Thomas Chase, the authorities gathered at the same spot for another interment, that of an infant, Samual Brewster Ames. After the church services for the child, a delegation of church and civil authorities hastened to the vault to examine its seals. They found the cement which held the huge capstone intact. The vault, which had been under guard for four years, showed no signs of tampering.

But inside it was a different story. The bewildered officials found the four coffins jumbled in the confines of the six-by-twelve-foot vault. The lead-sheathed casket of Thomas Chase, so heavy that eight men were required to lift it, was across the vault from where it had been left four years before, and turned over on its side. Only one of the four coffins was unchanged, that of Mrs. Goddard, the original occupant of the tomb.

Again the coffins were returned to their original positions and the entrance carefully sealed in the presence of many witnesses. The guard was placed within fifty feet of the vault with instructions to shoot anyone who approached it without authority. There had been entirely too much of this matter already; people were aroused and the officials were embarrassed.

Doubtless they were even more embarrassed when Samual Brewster was buried in the same vault only two months later. For in spite of their elaborate precautions the coffins were again found in confusion, which pretty well describes the predicament of the officials as well. The coffins were replaced, the vault carefully sealed with cement.

The following year Barbados got a new Governor, Field-Marshal Viscount Combermere, a hard-bitten old warrior who took no stock in such fantastic stories as galloping coffins. Twaddle and nonsense! Lord Combermere let it be bruited about that if any more tampering with graves took place, the guilty parties would find themselves dealing with a very severe and forthright fellow. Just in case, he quietly called in the Reverend Orderson and others to brief him on the matter.

Perhaps this explains how Lord Combermere, Governor of Barbados, happened to attend the funeral of Thomazina Clark on July 17, 1819. She was neither wealthy nor politically prominent in the affairs of the island, but she was of interest to the Governor and many other officials because she was to be interred in the strange Chase vault.

To the Governor and his aides-de-camp the interior of the vault was a most interesting spectacle—with the six coffins piled about helter-skelter. One of them, that of Mrs. Goddard, had either fallen apart or had been torn to bits. Being of wood, perhaps it had been unable to resist the same forces which had moved the other leaden coffins. The Governor ordered one of his aides to make a chart showing the positions in which the coffins were found as well as the positions to which they were returned. The seventh box, containing the mortal remains of the late Thomazina Clark, was carefully placed on top of the coffin of Samuel Brewster and then the vault was carefully examined and sounded for possible secret entrances, but none was found. The floor was covered with white sand carefully brushed out smooth, the steps lightly sprinkled with wood ash and the heavy stone slab cemented into place. To make doubly sure that his trap was set the Governor and his aides placed their seals in the cement.

The term of Lord Combermere as Governor of Barbados was drawing to a close in 1820, and before he left the island he wanted to assure himself that he had scotched the nonsense about the Chase vault. Accordingly he served noticed that, because of sounds that had reportedly been heard in the old Christ Church cemetery, the Chase vault would be opened on April 18th.

The seals in the cement were unbroken. The heavy stone slab was freed and carefully slid back. The Governor assured himself that the wood ashes on the steps bore no marks of an intruder—but inside the vault itself the coffins were loosely stacked in a pile. Only the cloth sack containing the remains of Mrs. Goddard stood in a corner where it had been placed a few months before. Most baffling of all, the coffins themselves were reversed in position with the heads towards the door of the vault, a rather difficult thing to accomplish since the vault was so narrow that the Governor and his men had to take the coffins outside to turn them round.

Lord Combermere left Barbados in 1820, subsequently recording in his memoirs one of the fullest accounts of the restless dead in the Chase vault. The surviving members of that family decided that enough was enough and they removed the bodies to another cemetery where they might rest in peace. The original Christ Church was destroyed by a hurricane in 1831. Its successor was destroyed by fire in 1935.

The Chase vault still stands, its heavy stones and coral intact. No longer in use, its face stone has been subjected to the indignities inflicted by ignorant visitors, one of whom has scarred its surface with a symbol that seems peculiarly appropriate—a huge question mark.

Similar in many respects to the mystifying events at the Chase vault is the much more recent chronicle of August 24th, 1943. On that date the Masons of Barbados gathered at the tomb of Sir Evan MacGregor, who had been buried there in 1841. The Masons were not interested in Sir Evan, but in one Alexander Irvine, the father of Freemasonry in Barbados, who had been buried in the same vault prior to MacGregor.

In keeping with the respect due to Irvine, a select group of fellow Masons arrived at the old churchyard in August of '43 to be on hand when the vault was opened.

Like the Chase vault, this one had been carved out so that it was partly underground. It was solidly constructed of thick stone surmounting a cemented brick base which extended underground to a depth of about four feet. Entrance was obtained by descending a flight of six steps and opening a sealed door. After the heavy cover slab had been removed, it was found that the doorway to the vault itself had been bricked up.

As the bricks were removed the workmen called the attention of the Masonic delegation to a metal object of some sort that was visible through the opening that had been made. A little more careful work and the nature of the metal object became plain—it was a coffin sheathed in lead, leaning against the bricked-up door, head downward. Little by little the bricks were taken out, and the coffin slid away from the door until it rested on the floor.

The Masons were understandably mystified. How did this lead coffin, containing the remains of Sir Evan MacGregor, get out of its niche in the side of the vault and assume an upright position against the bricked-up door? What had moved it after the vault had been sealed more than a hundred years before? And what had produced the three tiny holes in the lid where it was soldered to the side?

The Masonic delegation found all this very confusing, of course, but they could not devote much time to the matter—for there was no trace of either the coffin or the body of Alexander Irvine, whose remains had occupied a niche in the vault when Sir Evan was placed beside him.

Empty-handed and baffled, the Masons re-sealed the tomb of Sir Evan MacGregor and went away to ponder the unexplained disappearance of Alexander Irvine, whose remains should have been in the sealed tomb where they had been placed, except that they were not there and no one knows why.

The strange disturbances in the Chase vault at Barbados are by no means the only instances of their kind on record. There is, for instance, the case of the French family vault in the church-yard at Stanton, in Suffolk, England. According to the church records, the burials in this vault consisted of placing the coffins on stout wooden biers. There was considerable astonishment when the vault was opened in 1755 and the coffins were found to be disarranged. One of them, a large lead-covered box which required eight men to lift, was discovered on the side of the vault opposite the bier which had originally held it, and the coffin was lying tilted on the fourth step of the stairs which led down into the vault. As in the Barbadian disturbances, the seals on the door were intact and there was no evidence that flooding had occurred.

The island of Oesel in the Baltic is small, windswept and rocky. It is best known for the whiskey it exports and for the unsolved mystery of the Arensburg graves.

Arensburg is the only town on the island. It is customary for the wealthier families to build private chapels where the heavy oak coffins can be kept for a time before they are transferred to the adjoining vault for final burial.

A highway runs alongside the cemetery, and from this road several of the private chapels are visible. One of them, owned by the Buxhoewden family, is nearest the road and it was in it that the puzzling disturbances were recorded.

The American minister to Naples, Robert Dale Owen, made the matter the subject of a lengthy report, basing it on the testimony of the family of Baron de Guldenstubbé, one of the principals involved.

Briefly, here is what reportedly occurred:

On Monday, June 22nd, 1844, the wife of a tailor named Dalmann drove to the cemetery to visit the grave of her mother. She had her two small children with her in the cart and she hitched the horse to a post in front of the Buxhoewden chapel. When she returned to the cart a few minutes later, she found the horse in a very excited condition, heavily lathered and evidently in a state of terror. Unable to drive the animal in that condition, the woman brought a veterinarian who promptly applied the universal remedy of those days—he bled the horse.

Mrs. Dalmann made a trip to tell her story to Baron de Guldenstubbé at his château near Arensburg. He was polite, but unimpressed by this incident of an excited old mare.

On the following Sunday several persons who had tied their horses to the Buxhoewden chapel came from the services to find their animals in a state of trembling and terror. A few days later villagers who passed by the spot frequently reported that they heard heavy rumbling sounds from the vault below the family chapel. More animals became frightened at the same spot and in the same fashion as Mrs. Dalmann's horse. Something very unusual was taking place there, of that the officials were agreed—but what was it?

There was so much talk and so much exaggeration that something had to be done. Perhaps an official investigation—to bring this troublesome incident to an end once and for all. At first the Buxhoewden family opposed the idea of a probe, contending that the whole thing was probably some scheme by an enemy of the family who wished to make them look silly. Before they would consider any request to let officials open the vault, several members of the family visited the place to assure themselves that all was in order. Instead, they found the coffins piled in the centre of the vault floor. The family inspection party patiently lifted all the coffins back into place on the iron racks around the walls, locked the door and poured lead into the seals as an extra precaution against tampering.

For a few days there were no additional reports of any weird noises from the chapel. Then, on the third Sunday in July, the storm broke again.

Eleven horses were tethered in front of the Buxhoewden chapel while their owners attended services. Passers-by found the horses plunging and rearing for no apparent reason, in some cases throwing themselves violently to earth as they sought to break their hitching lines. By the time the alarm was spread, six of the horses were down and could not get up; the others were 'saved' by that standard procedure, bleeding. Three of the horses died where they lay—whether from the fright or the bleeding is not known.

Those who had lost their horses in this peculiar incident were joined by other angered and alarmed citizens in a plea to the Consistory—a church court which sat periodically at Arensburg. The Consistory could not decide what to do—if anything—and while it dawdled, Fate took a hand in the matter.

There was a death in the Buxhoewden family, and after the funeral services several members of the family decided to visit the vault beneath the chapel. They discovered that all of the coffins were piled in a heap in the middle of the floor. They laboriously lifted them back in place on the heavy iron racks and locked the door, pouring lead into the seals as an extra precaution.

Word got around that there was something very strange taking place in and around that particular chapel. The rumours became so exaggerated and so persistent that the Consistory was forced to take action and, like most committees, their first thought was to investigate. The Buxhoewdens still opposed any probe, taking the position that the whole thing was the work of some enemy of theirs who sought to embarrass them before the public. But upon second thought they changed their minds: After all, hadn't they just replaced the coffins and sealed the doors? What better time for an investigation than that moment?

They reckoned without their riddle.

Baron de Guldenstubbé, President of the Consistory, visited the vault with two of the Buxhoewdens. Again they found the seals unbroken, the coffins piled in the middle of the vault. They replaced the coffins and re-sealed the doors. The die was cast: there must be an investigation of this matter at once.

The committee which was chosen for the job consisted of Baron de Guldenstubbé, a Bishop, a Doctor Luce, two members of the Consistory, the burgomaster and another town official and a secretary to take down what was seen and said.

The committee found the seals on the vault intact. They also found the coffins, with the exception of a grandmother and two small children, again piled up in the centre of the vault.

Had the purpose of the repeated intrusions (three such incidents in five weeks) been robbery? None of the coffins showed any sign of tampering, but just to be on the safe side the committee opened a couple and found jewellery intact. The robbery motive was worthless.

How had the intruders entered?

Since the door seals had not been disturbed, the committee suspected that a tunnel might have been dug. They dug up the floor in a vain search for a secret entrance; they dug trenches around the vault with no more success. Baffled, the dignitaries on the investigating body decided that there could have been only one means of entrance and that must have been through the locked doors of the vault. Accordingly they scattered fine wood ashes over the floor of the crypt, locked and sealed the door, and sprinkled more wood ashes on the steps leading up to the chapel.

Guards from the city staff were posted twenty-four hours per day for seventy-two hours to keep everyone away from the troublesome tomb.

At the end of the three-day waiting period the Consistory committee returned. According to Owen they found both doors sealed and locked, and upon opening them they found the wood ashes undisturbed. And the coffins? They were tumbled about the vault, some of them even standing on end. Only the coffin that contained the grandmother and those of the two children were unchanged.

The committee assured itself once more that robbery had not been involved and that there was no secret entrance. Then the coffins were removed for burial elsewhere. In Arensburg, as in Barbados, that seemed to be the only means of bringing peace to the restless dead.

Odd Jobs

WHAT would you do with a hundred barrels of porcupines? Would you buy them at two dollars a barrel? Neither would I; but that's why we are where we are today; and that's why Cliff Tagere of Boston is a wealthy man. He bought the porcupines.

It is well that he did, because Cliff had an idea. He had hundreds of thousands of quills at his disposal in those barrels. So he simply took a few of the quills, attaching each one to the top of a postcard, and sent them to the presidents of insurance companies. The card said: 'This is a porcupine quill. The porcupine is the best protected animal in the woods. If he ever came to town and saw so many people without insurance, he would laugh himself to death.' Within a week Cliff had a contract to furnish a quarter of a million of his neat novelties to a big insurance company. He turned his barrels of porcupines into more than $60,000 before the fad was over. All because he had an idea to go with them.

That fellow with the porcupines brings to mind another true story about another well-known denizen of the woods, the lowly and much-maligned skunk. It all began when Mrs. Sadie Redekopp of Dallas, Oregon, discovered under her barn a long-haired black animal with white stripes. Even as we would have done she made tracks away from there and fast! From a safe distance she looked back. The anticipated gas attack had not materialized. Instead, four little baby skunks were peeking from under the barn, getting their first view of the world. To Mrs. Redekopp they were irresistible.

Perhaps other people would love them, too. She called up the neighbourhood veterinarian and inquired about the possibility of disarming the skunks. Could it be done? He assured her that it could, very simply. So she rounded up the babies and took them over to him. A week later they were home, completely neutralized, as the military men would say.

Mrs. Redekopp put an ad in the Dallas paper, offering harmless deodorized baby skunks at ten dollars apiece. Other newspapers picked it up as news, and Mrs. Redekopp was swamped with orders from all over the country. She couldn't meet the demand, so she in turn had to advertise in country weeklies over the backwoods areas, and soon the skunks and orders were coming out about even. Today she is the proprietor of a business that grosses about $80,000 a year, dealing exclusively in deodorized polecats, a business called 'Skunks, Incorporated'. She says that ninety per cent of the little fellows she sells for pets come up with the same name, a rank injustice under the circumstances. The kids call most of them 'Stinky'.

Charles Daniels of Balboa Heights in the Canal Zone is another fellow who made an idea pay off. Ten years ago he started to experiment with ordinary clover to see what makes it produce four-leaf clovers. He never did learn, but he finally developed a strain that turns up with four-leaf clovers ninety-nine times out of a hundred. If there is anything the world wants it is something that will bring good luck, and Charlie had thousands of the best-known talismans. In 1940 he sold $40,000 worth, and today he will gross more than $75,000 from his glorified front yard. He hires fifteen native girls to pick the plants and they work only in the early morning and late evening.

When Daniels first embarked on this hobby, he had no intention of commercializing. Then one day a friend of his left on a flying trip around South America. He was making the flight of necessity in an old tri-motor Ford plane, long past due for the junk pile, and over uncharted areas. He told Daniels he needed all the luck he could get and Daniels promptly gave him a handful of the four-leafed clovers. The trip was highly successful, and the friend spread the story of the clovers wherever he went. Orders began to roll in from all over South America, and the newspapers picked up the story of this unique enterprise.

Charlie says the largest order he ever sold was to an insurance company. They bought a million leaves, encased them in little plastic calendars which said: 'For good luck the whole year through, four-leaf clovers. For protection, traveller's insurance.'

Skunks, four-leaf clovers, and porcupines by the barrel, they all paid off to folks who had ideas.

Oak Island's Untouchable Treasure

In recent years the use of electronic devices for locating buried metal has merely confirmed what dozens of frustrated treasure-seekers already knew—the gold of Oak Island is there all right, defying all efforts to take it, just as it has for more than a hundred years.

It lured Dr. John Lynds to bankruptcy, just as it had lured hapless Tony Vaughan, Danny McGinnis and Jack Smith before him. And eventually the elusive treasure of Oak Island listed among its victims one Franklin D. Roosevelt and his friends.

Smith, Vaughan and McGinnis were the first to suspect that treasure was there, when they rowed over to the island one Sunday morning in 1795. They lived in Luneberg, in the southern part of Nova Scotia on Mahone Bay, which is an inlet of the ocean. Oak Island got its name from its stand of live oak trees, unusual in that latitude. In the days of the freebooters it was a haven of refuge and repair. What else it may have been is lost in the records, but there is considerable evidence to indicate that at some time some-one went to a great deal of trouble to conceal a treasure there—a treasure which is still there.

Jack Smith and his companions were not treasure-hunting at all when they rowed to the island for the first time. But when they noticed the huge oak trees, several hundred feet inland, with a sawed-off limb that showed signs of having once supported a block and tackle, their curiosity was aroused. Moreover, directly beneath the tree there was a circular depression some ten or twelve feet in diameter. Had the tree been used to lower some very heavy object into a hole? The three young men could arrive at no other conclusion.

They hurried back to the mainland for spades and axes. On the following day they began their digging. It was hard work, for the clay was firmly packed. Were they chasing a will-o'-the-wisp? At the twelve-foot level they found their answer, a thin layer of stone which showed unmistakable marks of having been cut through by some earlier tools.

This was encouraging, but unprofitable in itself. They might have abandoned the search had they not uncovered another hint a few feet deeper: this time a thick layer which might have been a platform of tightly woven coconut fibre. At the twenty-two-foot mark they went through another layer of coconut fibre.

To the three excited young men it became apparent that they had embarked on a task which would require more manpower. They were down thirty feet, had gone through a layer of heavy oak planks into the hard clay again, with nothing to show for their weeks of backbreaking toil except calluses and clues. But those whom they approached with their story were not interested. It made no sense to them to believe that pirates or anyone else in possession of great wealth would go to such lengths to bury it on an out-of-the-way place like Oak Island.

Jack Smith married and built himself a home about two hundred yards from the pit which he and his friends had dug. For a total of seven years they struggled to sink that shaft a few feet deeper. Lacking adequate tools, they occasionally found that much of the work had to be done over again as braces collapsed and walls crumbled. But little by little they got down to about thirty-five feet by the summer of 1803.

That was when Smith took his wife to Luneberg to be attended by Dr. John Lynds when her first child was born. It

E

was a fateful occasion for the doctor, for Smith's stories of the strange pit on Oak Island intrigued the physician into becoming a partner in the venture.

Workmen were hired. The walls of the shaft were carefully braced. Winches lifted tons of earth and debris as the hole deepened, for at successive ten-foot levels more layers of coconut fibres, oak planks or ship's putty were found. At the ninety-foot level the diggers encountered a new factor. As they tore out the heavy layer of oak planking they exposed a flat stone tablet which bore unintelligible hieroglyphics. It was carefully preserved for years and shown to various scholars, none of whom had the faintest idea of the message it bore. Finally Smith took possession of it and embedded it in the facing of his fireplace, where it could be seen without being stolen. Long after his death it was taken to Halifax, where it eventually disappeared, still undeciphered.

The discovery of the strangely marked stone spurred Dr. Lynds and his friends on to greater effort. They had already seen enough to convince them that someone had gone to great time and expense to bury something at this remote place. Surely they could not be far from the treasure itself! At a hundred feet, the mark where they had been expecting to find their reward, they found only another and more massive layer of planks and ship's putty.

Dr. Lynds ordered a large drill to be driven through this latest impediment. The instrument slowly made its way through the hardwood and the brittle putty until it appeared to drop into some sort of subterranean room. There was a hasty conference at which it was decided to call a halt for the day because of darkness. Tomorrow, certainly, they would break through this last barrier into the chamber where the treasure was stored!

When morning came the workmen found their pit more than half filled with water. In desperation they bought pumping equipment which worked round the clock with little effect. If they lowered the level by evening, it had regained its former depth by morning.

Desperate men take desperate measures. Dr. Lynds and his indefatigable treasure-seekers decided to sink another shaft alongside the one that was filled with water. Working with an energy enlivened by the belief that they were within reach of their exciting goal, they sank this second shaft to a depth of one hundred and ten feet. This, they reasoned, put them below the room which contained the presumed treasure. Just dig a lateral into the room, or beneath it, loot it of its riches, and the job would be done.

They had overlooked one basic law of nature—the eagerness with which water seeks its own level. As they started cutting their lateral the water from the old shaft broke through in a flood. Three of the workmen drowned. The dazed and battered survivors now had two holes filled with water to show for their years of work and the vast sums of money they had spent. They were bankrupt and defeated and they sadly faced the facts.

In the ensuing forty-six years the treasure of Oak Island lapsed into the status of a legend to be discussed and laughed at around the fire on long winter nights. But to Dr. John Lynds it was no legend. To him it was very real and very near, almost within his grasp, until that infernal water came in.

In 1849, when the gold madness in California was driving men out of their minds, Dr. Lynds saw his chance to strike again. Old now, and rheumy-eyed, but still full of fire when he talked about Oak Island, the doctor managed to gather about him a new group of financial backers and they went to work at the site of the original shaft—the one begun fifty-four years before by Smith, Vaughan and McGinnis. In the intervening years it had filled in, of course, but the debris was loose and progress was rapid.

At one hundred and ten feet, ten feet deeper than Lynds had been able to sink the same shaft, they struck what seemed to be a layer of solid stone.

Stone? Dr. Lynds did not remember any stone below that first shaft. Perhaps it was time to sink another drill to determine what they could expect if they continued their excavating.

They used what was known as a 'pod' drill, considered to be a very efficient device for such matters, since it contained a trough which would bring up samples with a bit of luck.

The big auger, slowly turned by hand, made its way through a layer of stone or hard plaster, then into about a foot of empty space before it touched wood. Four inches of wood, and the workmen excitedly announced that they could feel the end of the bit turning in some sort of loose metal. For nearly an hour they probed as best they could with the drill tip, but it refused to work its way through the metal which apparently encased it.

There were five workmen in the bottom of the shaft when the drill came up to be inspected by flickering candlelight, but all five of them reportedly yelled at the same time. There, twisted about the screw tip on the drill and jammed into its pod, were three heavy gold links, unquestionably part of a chain!

Then once again water rushed in and ruined the shaft. This time no one was killed, and when work was resumed the following summer the backers of the scheme had hired some engineers to plan the thing more effectively.

These engineers were very practical men and they were experienced in such matters. One of the first things that occurred to them was the improbability of the hard clay's letting in such vast quantities of water in such a short period of time. They also noticed that the water in the shafts rose and fell with the nearby tide. Therefore, they reasoned, the water in the shafts came not from the clay but from the sea, through some underground passage.

Further drilling in the nearest inlet confirmed their suspicions. There was ample evidence that a cofferdam had been built while a tunnel had been dug from the inlet to the spot where the treasure room seemed to be located, a matter of four hundred feet. The engineers reasoned that after the treasure had been stowed away, a thick layer of coconut matting had been placed over the entrance to the tunnel and the matting covered with sand and clay before the cofferdam was opened to flood the place and conceal the entrance. They found traces of the matting but they could not find the tunnel they sought.

If the tides were connected with the water-filled shafts, then the connection could be discovered by putting quantities of bright dyes in the shafts and letting them seep out into the inlet. The red dyes seeped out, after several days, just about where the engineers expected to find the tunnel's mouth, at a point called Smith's Inlet.

On the basis of this evidence the company took the last of its funds and built a huge cofferdam. Once this was completed they would be in a position to pump out the water behind it, rip off the mass of rocks and debris which concealed the tunnel's mouth, and make their way to the treasure which dangled just out of reach.

Again disaster struck when success seemed to be at hand. With most of their money spent and only three days' work to be completed on the cofferdam, a huge wave came roaring in and demolished all that they had accomplished.

In 1865 still another group tried their hand at tapping the Oak Island treasure, with no more success than Dr. Lynd had managed. The next attempt was in 1874, when a group of New York business men spent almost a hundred thousand dollars pumping water and telling each other they were just about to find the treasure. But they, too, were defeated by the apparently inexhaustible flood that poured into the shaft.

Since the days of Dr. Lynds' valiant probing there has been only one noteworthy development at Oak Island. In 1893 an insurance man named Frederick Blair arrived on the scene with plenty of money and some good engineers. They decided that it was easier to drill through water than to pump it out. If the drills brought up any proof that there was treasure down there, Mr. Blair would proceed. If the drills failed to produce any evidence, he would pack up and go home, with his and his backers' money unspent.

Unfortunately for Mr. Blair and his friends, the drill brought up three very interesting bits of evidence: First, it showed unmistakable signs of having drilled through gold; second, it indicated that there were layers of wooden casks or boxes filled with gold to a depth of at least thirty feet and that these containers were in a room made of heavy lumber and coated with crude cement about twenty inches thick; third, one of the drills brought up a tiny scrap of what appeared to be parchment, which bore the letters 'W' and 'I'.

Convinced that something was there, something well worth retrieving, Blair and his company spent a fortune in a futile try at the treasure. With dyes poured into the shafts, they found that *two* tunnels had been bored to protect the treasure, one leading to the nearest inlet, the other showing up several hundred yards away in another cove. After four years of sinking shafts, the syndicate had to admit defeat. Only Blair had faith that the jinx of Oak Island could be licked, and he struggled doggedly on until 1905, when poverty overtook him.

Franklin D. Roosevelt was a frequent summer visitor at Campobello, just across the Bay of Fundy from Nova Scotia. He and some friends decided to have a try at the elusive Oak Island treasure and they formed a company which began operation in August of 1909. They spent the summer there, and they spent some money, but all they took with them were some wonderful memories.

The latest operator on the Oak Island scene is a retired steel magnate, Gilbert Hedden, who, like Frederick Blair, brought to the task a generous supply of money and modern equipment in 1935. After desultory operations for a few years, Hedden decided that it had been a wonderful experience, but the treasure of Oak Island was still untouched after more than 150 years of defying all comers.

There are two theories which may explain what lies at the bottom of the pits on Oak Island and how it got there.

Both concern themselves with the French crown.

The supposition to which the late President Roosevelt adhered concerned itself with the crown jewels of Louis XVI.

According to this version, a lady-in-waiting fled with the jewels while the King was busy trying to save his neck. It is known that such a person did reach Louisburg, a French fort a few miles north of Oak Island, but precisely what she brought with her in the way of baggage is not a matter of any existing record unless the record is buried on Oak Island.

The other hypothesis, and the one which is given most credence by those who have devoted a great deal of time to this puzzle, deals with the known fact that in the middle of the eighteenth century, when France was wrangling with England over claims in the New World, the French government decided to make Fort Louisburg into an impregnable base of operations and ten million dollars in gold was sent for that purpose. It is a matter of record that the gold arrived at Louisburg. It is also a matter of record that the corrupt Governor spent only a small portion of that sum in improving the fortifications. Students of history have been unable to find any indication that the Governor sent the balance back to his sovereign.

The futile attempts to bring up the treasure of Oak Island have established certain things to be true, in the opinion of the engineers. There is some sort of cement and wood chamber which contains gold. The persons who concealed this gold did so by lengthy and extremely clever feats of engineering performed at heavy expense over a considerable period of time. They evidently built cofferdams, tunnelled under the island, placed the treasure in its specially built chamber and filled in the pit through which the weighty casks were lowered. Then, according to the opinions of the engineers, the tunnels connecting the treasure room with the sea were sealed over by layers of coconut fibres weighted down with rocks and covered with sand, achieving a watery trap for anyone who did not know where to find and plug the entrances to the tunnels before trying to enter the treasure chamber itself.

If this hypothesis is correct, then the treasure of Oak Island was placed there as part of a long-range high-level plan. For some reason, possibly the collapse of the regime and the death of its leaders, the treasure was never recovered. Will it ever be brought to light?

Nobody knows. But it lies there today just as it has for a century and a half, tantalizing modern treasure-hunters by buzzing their electronic metal-finding devices—just as its shreds of gold chain teased the diggers of years gone by. The treasure is there . . . and it is as elusive as ever.

They Cheated the Hangman

THE crowd ceased its growling and became ominously silent as the nine young men came tramping across the cobblestoned street which led from the prison to the courthouse. They were leaders of the Young Ireland disorders, convicted of treason against the Queen, and they were surrounded by soldiers and chained together like common felons. The year was 1848. The penalty for their crime was death.

Except for Her Majesty's officials and the prisoners, the courtroom was empty. These men must be dealt with firmly; the spirit of rebellion which they represented must be scotched without further delay. The presiding judge cleared his throat and began:

'Patrick Donahue, Charles Duffy, Thomas McGee, John Mitchell, Thomas Meagher, Terence McManus, Michael Ireland, Morris Lyene and Richard O'Gorman, you have been tried and found guilty of treason against the Crown. Have you anything to say before the court passes sentence?'

Thomas Meagher had been chosen by the group to be their spokesman. It was a warm spring day and the windows of the court were open. He knew that the crowd, which stood silently outside, could hear him.

Meagher's statement to the court was delivered in clear,

ringing tones which carried out to the crowd, as the judge well knew.

'Your lordship,' he said, 'this is our first offence, but not our last. If you can find it possible to be easy with us this once, sir, we pledge our word as gentlemen that we will do better next time. And the next time we will not be fools enough to get caught!'

A roar of applause poured in from the crowd outside. The irate judge flushed crimson and banged his gavel for order. He promptly sentenced them to be hanged to death.

The story of the nine young Irish leaders spread around the world and caught the popular fancy. Protests engulfed the British government, and Queen Victoria found it inadvisable to carry out the death sentence on these courageous young men. Instead, she ordered the sentence commuted to life imprisonment in the penal colonies of what was then the wild and uninviting land of Australia.

They were just what Australia needed; the men and the moment had arrived together. Patriots and fearless, they soon bade farewell to the penal colony and turned their undesirable talents to more fruitful pursuits.

John Mitchell made his way to the United States and had a brilliant career in the politics of New York State; his son became Mayor of New York City. Tom McGee rose swiftly to become an esteemed member of the Canadian House of Commons. Thomas McManus and Patrick Donahue became brigadier-generals in the Union Armies during the Civil War. Richard O'Gorman became the Governor-General of Newfoundland. Tom Meagher became Governor of Montana.

Three of the original nine spent their careers in the land to which they had been exiled. Morris Lyene served as a brilliant Attorney-General of Australia, winning many a legal tilt against the British barristers, and Lyene was succeeded in that office by his old fellow prisoner, Michael Ireland.

Bitterest pill of all for Queen Victoria came in 1871 when she found herself dealing with the newly elected Prime Minister of

Australia, Mr. Charles Duffy. To her amazement and distress, the Queen learned that this was the same Charles Duffy who had been exiled for high treason twenty-three years before. When the records of the other eight compatriots of Duffy were brought to the Queen, she seemed pleased. Perhaps she realized at last that by cheating the hangman she had enriched humanity.

Therese Neumann—A Living Riddle

On Good Friday of 1956 a crowd of several thousand persons gathered in the street before the home of a humble peasant woman in Konnersreuth, Germany. In the throng were those who had flown hundreds of miles to be there on that particular day. They mingled with the curious and the sceptics as well as with the devout. One and all they had a common aspiration—to get a glimpse of Therese Neumann, a living mystery and one of the most baffling that medical science has ever sought to explain.

Whatever their motives in seeking to see Miss Neumann at that particular time, they were doomed to disappointment. For inside the cottage the famed stigmatist suffered in seclusion, her agonies witnessed only by the surviving members of her immediate family and by the aged parish priest, eighty-four-year-old Father Naber, who has been her constant friend and counsellor since the inception of her strange experiences.

Therese Neumann is a stigmatist, a person whose body displays wounds similar in location and nature to those suffered by Christ on the cross. Each year since these wounds made their first appearance on her body in Holy Week of 1926, Therese has undergone this ordeal, which reaches its most active stage on Good Friday. While there have been many other stigmatists (some of them are still living at the present time), the case of Miss

Neumann seems to be typical and is probably the most widely known.

She was twenty-eight years old in 1926 when her strange story began. A wound appeared on her left side, directly over the heart, and began to bleed copiously. (The spear wound in Christ's body was on the right side.) Therese managed to conceal her injury from her parents for a couple of days, but by Good Friday further concealment was impossible. She was bleeding from wounds around the crown of her head and from small round holes which had appeared on each of her hands and feet.

Her frightened parents called their parish priest, Father Naber, who instantly recognized the stigmata. He made a careful note of what he saw, adding that in addition to the wounds near the heart, and on the head, hands and feet, Miss Neumann was also bleeding from the eyes. Dr. Otto Seidl from nearby Waldsassen was called, but only after home remedies had failed to heal the condition. The doctor made a careful examination of the conditions, and his report states that the wound near Therese's heart was about one and a half inches long. Covering the bleeding spots with a salve, the mystified physician went away—the first of a long line of medical experts who came and saw and were confounded.

Miss Neumann continued to suffer excruciating pain from her wounds until about three o'clock on the morning of April 17th, when she prayed for relief. Suddenly, she says, she could feel the pain diminish and then it vanished altogether. She awakened her parents and when they removed the bandages they discovered that the wounds had healed without leaving scars. But another odd condition had ensued: the red flesh inside the wounds was visible through the dry transparency which covered them. Dr. Seidl was hurriedly summoned and his report says: 'This is a most extraordinary case. These wounds do not fester, nor do they become inflamed. There is not the slightest possibility of fraud as some have claimed.' Before he left, the doctor took new measurements of the baffling stigmata. He found that the wound on her side had not changed in size and that, like the other marks, it was glazed over. On her hands and feet the wounds were about the size of a sixpence.

Medically, her condition remained unchanged until June of 1927, when the marks on the tops of her hands and feet were duplicated inside her palms and on the soles of her feet, giving the appearance to the doctor and the priest of injuries which extended entirely through those parts. Examination later showed such injury had actually occurred. The location and nature of these wounds made walking difficult, and the sufferer found it impossible to grasp anything firmly with her hands.

The Bishop of Regensburg requested Miss Neumann to submit to a fifteen-day period of medical observation, to which she agreed. From July 14th to July 28th inclusive, in 1927, she underwent a series of the tests. During that period she was never without an attendant; one or another of the Mollersdorfer Sisters, members of a nursing order, lived with her in her home. Before and after the observation period, the Sisters were placed under oath by the Regensburg ordinariate. The Sisters were well qualified for the work of watching Miss Neumann and of reporting what they observed to Dr. Seidl under whose supervision the tests were conducted.

The record shows that his instructions were explicit and were carefully observed by the Sisters in attendance. Therese was not required to attend confession during this period. She was not bathed in the customary manner but was sponged lightly with a damp cloth. Not for a moment was she permitted to be alone. Since her reported ability to exist for long periods of time without food or water was part of the test, even the water for her mouth-wash was carefully weighed and measured both before and after using. The subject of the tests was not even permitted to empty or to handle in any way the small aquarium in the room, to obviate the possibility that she might secure extra water in this fashion.

According to the subsequent testimony of the Sisters and the doctors, Therese Neumann was a most unusual patient.

Dr. Ewald testified that although she had taken neither food nor water during the fourteen days of the test, she weighed exactly the same on July 28th as she had weighed on July 14th. At one time, during the profuse bleeding of the ecstasy, her weight had dropped six pounds, but she quickly regained this. Dr. Ewald pointed out that the body loses about 400 grams of water per day through normal processes. Although Miss Neumann took neither food nor water during her fourteen-day test period, she showed no signs of dehydration nor of hunger.

Even more remarkable than Dr. Ewald's testimony was that of Dr. Seidl, who had been Miss Neumann's attending physician for years at the time he told the Munich court under oath on April 15, 1935, that he was convinced that Therese took neither food nor water during the test period and that she had abstained from these items for much longer periods without injury to her health. This prolonged abstinence of their vital requirements cannot be explained naturally, said Dr. Seidl.

Instead of quieting the controversy which centred around Miss Neumann, the test period and the subsequent statements served only to solidify the respective contentions of the opposing viewpoints. On October 4, 1927, the Regensburg Diocese published an official statement which said in part:

'During the fifteen-day, day-and-night uninterrupted observation, not the least taking of nourishment occurred. Nor was Therese Neumann abed at all times, but was usually up. Completely puzzling was the fact that, despite the absolute fasting, twice after not inconsiderable losses of weight there followed approximately the same gains in weight. An observation in a clinic could not have had a more successful result.'

The Regensburg statement did not satsify the critics and doubters who sought a more naturalistic answer to the riddle of Therese Neumann. Doctors made the point that going without food for fifteen days was not unheard of—there have been many instances where persons have gone without food for thirty days or more and survived with no apparent ill-effects. But total abstinence from liquids for that same fifteen-day period presented a more baffling problem, for such a state of affairs presents a condition that would, by medical standards, end in certain death.

Had Therese Neumann abstained from liquids during her two-week test?

The Sisters and the two attending physicians agreed that she could not have obtained any liquid without their knowledge— and that she *had* abstained.

The doctors were not convinced. They pointed out that the test had been conducted in her own home, under conditions and controls which they were unwilling to accept as entirely neutral. Their insistence was so prolonged that the Church authorities at Regensburg suggested to Miss Neumann's father that a controlled test away from home might be advisable. The father refused to grant his permission, Therese accepted his decision, and there the matter was dropped.

The records of orthodox medicine have been used to support the claims of Miss Neumann's critics, who assert that her stigmata are the result of prolonged self-hypnosis. They point out that in many persons the power of the mind over the body is so great that they have been able to produce remarkable changes in the body by simply willing the changes to be made. Self-induced warts and blisters are not unusual, they say, and the critics go on to assert that stigmatists, by devoting so much time and thought to the desire for bleeding marks to appear, might well be able to bring them about.

Defenders of the stigmatists are not unanimous in their belief that the basis of the bleeding marks is entirely supernatural, yet they find certain unexplained aspects of the matter which have not been answered by naturalistic means.

In the recorded history of Therese Neumann (and of many other stigmatists) there are numerous occasions where she has apparently taken upon herself the sufferings of others who were relieved of their agonies at precisely the time hers began. There was the case of a young priest who had a severe throat ailment; of a miner who suffered from an ulcerated leg; of a young woman who had tried to commit suicide and who was in agony from the acid. In these cases, and in many others, Therese accepted their sufferings and they were instantly relieved, although some of them did not know of her intercession on their behalf. That she might be willing to control her own condition is conceivable, but conventional medicine has no explanation as to how she might at the same time control the mental and physical condition of others who knew nothing of her acts.

In an article published in the *American Weekly* in October 1939, the author, identified as psychiatrist Maurice Chideckel, brushed off the case of Therese Neumann as one of religious hysteria, combined with autographism and dermographism. These latter terms, he explained, dealt with the ability of some persons, under great emotional strain, to make marks on their bodies which would persist, he said, for unusually long periods of time: '. . . for weeks perhaps'. At that time Therese Neumann's wounds had been bleeding for *thirteen years*.

And what of the strange phrases which Therese used during her ecstasies, the words in long-dead tongues which she muttered from time to time as she tossed on her bed of pain?

Dr. Chideckel had a ready reply: Therese had heard Greek or Latin phrases during services at her church and had retained these words in the indelible subconscious mind, although she was not aware that she was storing them away.

The learned man's 'explanation' does not explain, for the strange words and phrases muttered by the stigmatist were Aramaic, which was current in the lifetime of Jesus but long since discarded. Where or how Therese Neumann acquired such words is beyond the knowledge of those closest to her, but one thing is certain—she never heard them spoken in her church or anywhere else.

Careful examination of Therese Neumann has established the following irrefutable facts: Since 1926 she has borne open wounds on her hands, feet, head and side. Each year, immediately prior to Good Friday, these wounds begin to bleed and the bleeding continues at least through Holy Week, sometimes a few

F

days longer. Microscopic examination, according to testimony of various physicians, confirms that the exudation from her wounds is blood and that it begins to flow spontaneously. The wound over the heart does not discharge blood but exudes a bloody serous substance—that is, a mixture of blood and other body fluids. The flow from the eyes is in such quantity that it could not be brought about by artificial means without leaving scar tissue of detectable extent.

Therese Neumann, the simple peason woman of Konners-reuth, is a stigmatist. The literature on stigmatists is voluminous, for more than three hundred such enigmatic cases have been recorded since St Francis of Assisi bore the marks of the cruci-fixion. There are other stigmatists living contemporaneously with Therese Neumann, as for instance the famed Padre Pio of Italy. Like her, they constitute living question marks for which science has found no mundane answers.

International Iceman

LIFE as we know it is possible on earth because of one simple fact which is seldom appreciated: the fact that ice is lighter than water.

If ice were heavier than water it would sink and millions of years ago the oceans would have become solid masses of ice with only a few shallow pools of water where the equatorial sun managed to thaw it out a bit. There would be no clouds, no rain, no life.

Fortunately nature has arranged things so that ice is lighter than water, with results which are readily apparent. Life, which began in hot water, is, in a manner of speaking, still in it.

Indirectly, it was the absence of ice which led to the discovery of America, for in the days of Columbus there was no artificial refrigeration. The food was either dried, salted, sugared or eaten fresh. The menus were monotonous, of course. Since much of their food was either rancid or spoiled, it had to be heavily spiced to conceal the flavour of semi-decay. This super-spicing led to widespread misery as the human body tried to defend itself, and it also led to a highly profitable trade in spices, a trade for which all nations scrambled.

Columbus was looking for a short route to the Spice Islands when he stumbled into the Caribbean at Queen Isabella's expense. Having no refrigeration, she sought spices. You might say that

Columbus discovered America because Queen Isabella had no icebox.

Spice continued to be used as a food preservative until well into the nineteenth century when a young Yankee began lugging blocks of ice around the world only to find that his prospective customers didn't know what he was talking about.

His name was Fredric Tudor. As a kid he had sat in the harbour at Boston and watched the schooners glide away on billowing sails for the far corners of the world. Like all kids he dreamed of adventure with a good ship underfoot and sails spanking in the breeze. The sailors told him stories of the unbearable heat of the tropics where the pitch oozed out of the deck seams. Fredric listened and slowly his dream took shape; he would some day conquer that equatorial heat with the abundance of ice which New England could furnish.

It was a grandiose dream that would require his full time, so Fredric Tudor quit Harvard in 1805 to make it come true.

For several months each winter the ponds around Boston were frozen solid. Getting the ice was no problem, but getting it to those suffering millions in the tropics was a very real problem.

Fredric chartered a schooner and loaded it with the last of his money. But once he got the stuff stowed away in the hold, his troubles began. Sailors wouldn't sign on his ship. It was foolish, they said, for the ice would melt and swamp the vessel. Shipping ice was nothing more than loading the ship with water from the inside; they would surely founder. Tudor wheedled and cajoled in vain. It took him ten days to round up a gang of wharf rats who were willing to risk their necks on this insane venture. One night, while Boston was sleeping, Tudor's vessel lifted anchor and steered out to sea on her way to Martinique.

Perhaps we should say that she started for Martinique. A few hundred miles out of Boston the ship encountered unseasonably warm weather, and the ice began to melt. Part of the crew mutinied and pulled for shore in a small boat. The rest of the men manned the pumps and sent the liquid cargo gushing overside. They did such a good job of pumping that by the time the ship reached Martinique there was little left to sell. Perhaps it was just as well, for the penniless natives there had nothing with which to buy. Tudor gave away what little ice remained and sailed back to Boston, loser by $4,500.

Obviously there was no money to be made trying to trade with people who had nothing with which to buy. Surely there must be somewhere in the world a nation where the people were both overheated and rich. The answer came to Tudor in a flash—India. There, he reasoned, lay the ideal combination of tropical heat and fabulous wealth. By borrowing from his friends, he drummed up another payroll, managed to lease another boat and loaded her with one hundred and thirty tons of highly perishable ice. All Boston turned out to see him off; newspapers wrote columns on what they described as 'Fredric's Folly'.

The little vessel fought every inch of the way down the Atlantic, around the Cape and back up to the Indian Ocean. By the time they finally docked in Calcutta half the ice had melted. Tudor had to act quickly or he was whipped. He stacked a sample cake of his ice on the pier. Thousands of Indians gathered round to see this strange stuff which had come so far. They came to see it but not to buy it; in fact, they could not be persuaded to touch it, for they didn't know what it was. A few of the hardier souls, the daredevils, screwed up enough courage to put their hands on it. They screamed and fainted, the crowd fled, and the ice dripped into the bay.

The Yankee iceman still wasn't whipped. He set up shop on the harbour front, just a modest little counter, and began serving cold drinks made from native fruit juices. Since he couldn't sell the stuff, he gave the drinks away free. The natives sipped the drinks cautiously, being careful not to touch the chunks of ice. But the idea took hold, and within a week every sailor on the ship had to be pressed into service at the counter to handle the mobs of thirsty Indians who milled around the drink stand. Tudor sold his ice, but he no more than broke even on the trip.

The international iceman had proved his point. He needed a market, and in order to get the market he had to do some consumer education. India was ready and there would be no more sales resistance there. So while another ship carried ice to Calcutta, Tudor took a load to Brazil where the formula of the ice drinks again worked like magic. Savannah, Mobile and New Orleans followed in that order. Tudor found that by insulating the vessels with thick layers of New England pine shavings he could cut the loss of the ice to a mere trifle. By offering samples he built a tremendous demand for his product; the 'Crazy Yankee' was able to laugh at his critics while he pocketed the lush profits.

Fredric Tudor, ice peddler *de luxe*, had sold an idea to the world. In his biggest year 363 shiploads of ice left Boston harbour for all parts of the globe. He was a king in his own realm, a position that he held for years until artificial ice machinery ruined the business.

By sticking to his own idea, Fredric Tudor became wealthy. But he died a poor man, the result of squandering his fortune speculating in coffee. He became the financial backer of a scheme to brew the coffee in Brazil and ship it to New York, ready to drink. As one critic said: 'He made a fortune selling cold water and lost it buying hot water.'

Fredric Tudor, the international iceman, was the perfect example of a super-salesman who finally bought a bill of goods.

None Came Back

ON land, sea and in the air men have vanished. Armies have marched into oblivion; great ships have disappeared without a trace; modern aircraft, equipped with the finest electronic safety devices, have flown into limbo.

Armies?

During the Spanish War of Succession (1701–1714) an army of four thousand trained and fully equipped troops marched into the foothills of the Pyrenees mountains and were never heard of again. In spite of numerous searches, no trace of them was ever found. They camped one night by a small stream. Next morning they broke camp and marched into the foothills, and oblivion.

In 1858 six hundred and fifty French troops vanished during a march on Saigon, in what is now Indo-China. There had been rioting in the city and five hundred hardy French Legionnaires, plus one hundred and fifty well-trained Spahis, were dispatched to restore order. They were seen marching across the open country about fifteen miles from Saigon, but they never reached the city and they never returned to their base. Like the missing Spaniards—they simply disappeared.

The Japanese sacked Nanking on December 10, 1939. Central China was in a panic, defences crumbling, chaos rampant.

It was imperative that the Japanese be delayed as long as humanly possible, for every hour counted to the beleaguered Chinese armies.

In the rolling foothills south of Nanking there was a natural fortress of sorts which could be used as the base for a desperate delaying action, provided troops could be got into position before the Japs arrived. The orders went out and a total of thirty-one hundred Chinese troops were rushed by train to a point some sixteen miles from the junction they were to guard. They quickly debarked, unlimbered their half-dozen howitzers and marched into position during the night. The commanding officer personally checked his men along a two-mile front to make certain that they were well dispersed (to reduce the effectiveness of anticipated aerial attack) and that they were dug in so that they could cover the road from Nanking with a minimum of casualties.

Colonel Li Fu Sien completed his tour of inspection at a few minutes past four in the morning. He went back to the truck that was his headquarters, parked in a tiny grove of trees two miles behind the lines. He had dozed off when an aide shook him into consciousness three hours later to inform him that headquarters was unable to contact the positions to the extreme right, as per his orders. The troops did not answer to the signals. What should be done?

Anything the Colonel might have suggested would have been too late, for every man on the line, with the exception of one small outpost, had simply disappeared. Their guns were still in place, in some cases their little fires were still glowing, when the search party made the rounds. There was no sign of a struggle and the sole remaining outpost had neither seen nor heard anything suspicious. If the army fled it could not have crossed over to the Japanese because the only bridge across the river was under scrutiny of the outpost that survived. All other escape routes were across open country which was virtually denuded of vegetation; there was no place for them to hide even from their own officers.

Did the missing troops surrender in a mass funk? There is no mention of it in the Japanese records of the campaign, and most significant perhaps is the fact that of the 2988 Chinese troops who vanished at that point, not one was ever seen or heard of again.

That is a dubious distinction they share with the crew and passengers of the stern-wheeler *Iron Mountain*, which was exactly eight years old the day she pulled in at Vicksburg in June of 1872. She was a brute of a river boat, 180 feet long, 35 feet wide, with five huge boilers to provide steam enough for her giant stern paddles. Loaded with cotton and molasses from New Orleans, she was bound for Pittsburgh.

With a couple of long blasts on her whistle to warn small boats out of the way, the *Iron Mountain* belched fire and smoke from her twin stacks as she swung her line of tow barges into the current and pulled round the bend.

What happened to her from that time on will probably never be known.

The first inkling that something was wrong came when another steamer, the *Iroquois Chief*, had to swing hurriedly across the river to get out of the way of a string of runaway barges. The *Chief* ran back down-river and picked up the tow-line. By dint of strenuous tugging, the barges were brought to a halt, but no boat showed up to claim them. And, oddly enough, the tow-line had not broken; it had been cut with an axe! This was common practice in case of emergency. Better to risk losing the barges in order to save the steamboat.

But what became of the *Iron Mountain*?

There was no debris, no trace of a fire or explosion and no indication that she sank from any cause. Along with her cargo and the fifty-five persons aboard, the *Iron Mountain* vanished without a trace.

The number of ships that have sailed away into oblivion is legion. When the oceans were trackless wastes where tiny sailing vessels ventured at the mercy of wind and wave, these disappearances were understandable. But in the twentieth century, to have modern steamships vanish with cargo and crew is quite another matter.

We need turn back no further than July 26th, 1909, when the new passenger liner *Waratah* steamed out of Durban, South Africa, with a full cargo of meat, flour and pig iron—and with two hundred and eleven persons aboard her. She was out of Australia for India and return; and now, twenty-six days after she left Sydney, she was starting the last leg of her journey.

The S.S. *Clan MacIntyre* saw her the following morning, churning down the coast towards Capetown and bucking heavy seas.

The *Waratah* was never seen again.

She disappeared as completely as if she had sailed off the earth —a sixteen-thousand-ton steamer, equipped with lifeboats, flares and rockets, that vanished without a trace along a shipping lane where eight other vessels were within sight of her rockets, had she fired any.

The Blue Anchor Line, which owned her, leased two ships, and the British government sent three warships into the area to search for ship or survivors. All craft using that part of the sea lane were alerted to watch for some evidence which might help solve the mystery. The search lasted for weeks, but not a plank, nor a life preserver, nor a body was ever found. The *Waratah*, like the four other ships before her which had borne that ill-fated name, had come to grief, but this time she had taken her secret with her.

The U.S.S. *Cyclops* left Barbados on March 4, 1918, bound for Hampton Roads, Virginia, with a crew of eighty-eight, a cargo of coal, and a rendezvous with oblivion. Like the *Waratah*, she vanished without a trace in an area that was well travelled. The *Cyclops* was a ship of the U.S. Navy and had full radio equipment —but when she encountered her final distress, she sent no messages. Just a trail of smoke over the horizon north of Barbados and the *Cyclops* was gone forever.

Of more recent vintage, but of the same degree of mystery, is the case of the Danish training vessel *Kobenhoven*. On the morning of December 14, 1928, the *Kobenhoven* took her leave of Monte-video after piping aboard her complement of fifty cadets and sailors. The youngsters had been taking part in a ceremony at the Danish consulate, little realizing that their future consisted of only a few hours. The *Kobenhoven* steamed out of the harbour, past a couple of small fishing vessels, and vanished. Whatever happened to her must have been almost instantaneous, for incoming ships, which sighted the same fishing vessels a few hours later, never saw the *Kobenhoven*.

The list of aeronauts who have vanished with their craft is long. The disappearance of balloons was not especially surprising, since they are at best children of the winds, man-made silken bubbles over which he has little control. Since the inception of ballooning the record has contained many instances where both man and balloon have slowly become mere specks in the sky—and question marks in the annals of the profession.

One of the question marks persisted for thirty-three years before it could be written off: Salomon August Andree, a Swedish explorer, believed that he could drift over the North Pole in a free balloon. With two companions he left Spitzbergen in his balloon on July 11, 1897, and vanished into the white nothingness to the north. Although numerous search parties scoured the Arctic and every clue was traced to its futile conclusion, Andree and his companions were not found until August 6, 1930, when their frozen bodies were located in the tattered remnants of their tiny tent—only 117 miles from their starting-point.

The case of Andree is an exception, of course: first, in that he was ever found at all; second, in that the canned bread and meats which he had taken with him were found to be unchanged after all those years. The bread was as fresh as the day he sailed away—and the films in his camera were finally developed to give the world a few pitiful glimpses of the explorers' last moments.

That Andree should fly into limbo for thirty-three years is understandable for the simple reason that he was risking his neck over a relatively desolate and unknown region without a means of communication from remote points.

How then can we explain the disappearance of fliers and planes on short flights over heavily populated terrain?

Albert Jewel owned one of the low-powered airplaines which were common to his time. On October 13, 1913, he took off from a small field at Hempstead, Long Island, for a flight of a few minutes' duration which was supposed to terminate on Staten Island. It was a clear day. The route he planned to fly included Jamaica and Coney Island. Mr. Jewel was simply going to take a little trip in his airplane over some of the most heavily populated areas in the nation and across a short stretch of the heavily travelled approach to one of the world's busiest harbours.

That was in 1913. Mr. Jewel never arrived at Staten Island, nor has he ever been heard of since.

Captain Mansell James flew from Lee, Massachusetts, on May 29th, 1919, with the announced intention of landing at Mitchell Field, Long Island. But, like Mr. Jewel, something detained him.

He was seen flying over the Berkshires, but he was never seen again. Five days later, after scores of search parties had found nothing, the Army sent planes into the area to fly over the same route in hopes of locating the wreckage. Nothing. Local newspapers carried reward notices; telephone companies called all their subscribers and alerted them to report at once any information which might lead to the discovery of the missing flier. Gradually the commotion died down. Captain James and his plane had flown away to nowhere and in the ensuing years they have been joined by many others.

It is noteworthy (if not significant) that many of these missing planes in recent years have made their last flights in a comparatively small area in the Atlantic north of Bermuda and bordered on the west from Florida to Virginia.

There have been others, of course, north of this zone. There was the unexplained disappearance of the French Latecoere 631, a huge flying boat capable of landing on the ocean, which vanished over the north Atlantic without a sign of its passing on August 1, 1948, carrying fifty-two persons to oblivion. And there was the U.S. C-124 with fifty-three aboard en route to Ireland on March 23, 1948, which disappeared over the north Atlantic. There must have been survivors, since a few life rafts were found, but the people were gone.

It was exactly one o'clock on the morning of January 30, 1948, when authorities at Kindley Field, Bermuda, sent out an alert for a plane which had been missing since ten-thirty of the preceding night. It was the British South American Airways four-engined luxury craft *Star Tiger* with twenty-three passengers and six crew members aboard. En route from Kingston, it had radioed, 'On course, four hundred miles from Bermuda, good weather and no trouble.' The plane and its human cargo simply vanished in the night. Ten ships of the U.S. Navy joined with thirty British and American planes in the fruitless search.

The *Ariel*, which Captain J. C. McPhee pulled off the runway at Bermuda at 7.45 a.m., January 17, 1949, was a sister ship of the ill-fated *Star Tiger*, which had vanished just about a year before. The *Ariel* had a crew of six, and thirteen passengers, and she expected to make the thousand miles to Kingston, Jamaica, in five hours and fifteen minutes. Just to be on the safe side, Captain McPhee had filled the tanks with enough fuel for ten hours of flight.

The last that was ever heard from the *Ariel* and its crew was a radio message forty minutes after it left Bermuda, when Captain McPhee reported that all was well and that he was changing his radio frequency to that of Kingston, a normal procedure.

Next morning the search was in full swing. Two American aircraft carriers were on the scene, the *Leyte* and the *Kearsage*, scanning the water to the north of Cuba. Three light cruisers, the *Portsmouth*, the *Huntingdon* and the *Fargo*, also assisted, as well as six destroyers.

South of Cuba, between that island and Jamaica, the mighty

U.S.S. *Missouri*, the light cruiser *Juneau* and four destroyers combed the seas. Two merchant ships turned from their travels to help in the hunt for the missing *Ariel*. Six Coast Guard PBMs flew over the area.

The net result of this great search was frustration.

The disappearance of the *Ariel*, like that of her sister ship the *Star Tiger*, was so sudden that the crew had no time to radio for help, and so complete that no trace was ever found.

As part of the routine pilot training at the Naval Air Station in Fort Lauderdale, Florida, the planes take off frequently for short triangular courses over the near-by ocean. It is customary for the fighter planes to follow a pre-determined flight plan which takes them eastward a given distance, where they make a sharp turn to cover the second leg of the course, eventually banking again and returning to base. On the afternoon of December 5, 1945, five TBM Avenger propeller-driven torpedo bombers left the base for one of these routine training flights. They were to fly 160 miles east over the ocean, forty miles north and then south-west back to the base. They had done it many times before, and there was no reason to believe that this trip was going to be different.

One plane carried two men; the others carried three each. All were equipped with the best radio and navigational equipment. All had self-inflating life rafts. Each man wore a life jacket.

At a few minutes past two o'clock in the afternoon the first Avenger roared down the runway and into the air. Six minutes later all five were in flight, cruising in formation over the rim of the Atlantic at something slightly in excess of two hundred miles per hour.

The first inkling of trouble came at three-forty-five. By that time the five planes should have been asking for landing instructions. Instead the base radio got a message from the flight leader which said: 'Can't be sure where we are. Can't see land. I'm not sure of our position.' All five of the navigators lost at the same time? Something incredible about that.

The misgivings at the base were well founded, for at four

o'clock the tower heard the planes talking anxiously among themselves—and heard the panicky flight commander turn the command over to another pilot. At four-twenty-five the last message trickled in: 'Still not certain where we are, but believe we are about 225 miles north-east of base. Looks like we are . . .' The voice trailed off into the silence which has engulfed both men and planes ever since.

Tragedy was obviously brewing and prompt emergency measures were called for. A big Martin Mariner flying boat, with a crew of thirteen, and loaded with rescue and survival equipment, roared out to the search—to guide the Avengers home, if possible.

Base radio flashed word to the Avengers that help was on the way. There was no reply.

Five minutes later base radio called the big flying boat to check its position. No reply.

The alarm was spread quickly. Coast Guard planes came roaring into action, following the flying boat's course towards the estimated position of the five missing torpedo bombers. Even after dark ten planes roamed the area, keeping a sharp lookout for a signal flare which they never saw. At dawn the escort carrier *Solomons* was on the scene, criss-crossing the sky from Florida to the Bahamas with her planes. In all, 240 planes were involved in this one operation, but not one of them ever found a trace of the six missing planes or their crews. Before the search was finally abandoned it had developed into the greatest air-sea rescue attempt on record, involving twenty-one ships, almost three hundred planes and twelve land parties that scoured the shores of the mainland and the islands for weeks, seeking some clue to the missing planes and crews.

The Naval Board of Inquiry, which met to conclude the case officially, considered all the known possibilities. The Avengers would have radioed an alarm had one or more of their group been forced down by accident or fuel shortage. Some of the men would almost certainly have escaped by taking to their parachutes. Debris of some sort would have been found had they crashed. Instead they merely vanished.

The big Martin flying boat could fly easily on one engine. It could land on the ocean. If its battery radio failed, it could still send messages on its hand-cranked set. Instead, it followed the five Avengers into the silence.

The Naval Board report says: 'We are not able to make even a good guess as to what happened.'

Also filed among the unexplained is the strange case of the Navy Super-Constellation, a sleek new passenger plane which took off from Patuxent, Maryland, to the Azores, on October 31, 1954, with forty-two persons aboard, many of them the wives and children of Navy personnel overseas. The plane was virtually brand new, equipped with two radio transmitters and all the necessary survival material in case it was forced down at sea. Like the five Avengers and the Martin flying boat, it just flew out into the silence which seems to engulf that portion of the middle Atlantic. Hundreds of ships and planes scoured the ocean for days without finding any evidence whatever which might solve the mystery of the missing plane or its passengers.

But if I were asked to cite the case which I regard as strangest of all, I would unhesitatingly turn to that of the twin-engined C-46 which crashed at the 11,000-foot level on Tahoma glacier in January of 1947. Rescue parties were dispatched immediately when the wreckage was located, for the plane had been carrying thirty-two persons, most of them military personnel, when it crashed.

Searchers found the crumpled plane on a slope of the glacier. They found the bloody bulkhead which bore mute evidence of the terrific impact when the ill-fated craft struck the mountain. And what of the thirty-two men aboard the plane? That is what the military would like to know—for, although rewards of five thousand dollars were offered for the discovery of the bodies, *not one of them was ever found.*

Another case where none came back.

Jumbo: Elephant Legend

On the ninth of April, 1882, a small sailing vessel churned the waters of the Hudson and battled her way to the pier where tens of thousands of people were waiting to greet her and her famous cargo.

Jumbo was coming to America. As Barnum said—'Jumbo, the biggest elephant that ever lived, mighty monarch of the jungle, proudest possession of the British Crown'—Jumbo was coming to America! But this morning the mighty monarch of the jungle was a mighty sick monarch. Nature had endowed him with great size and a friendly disposition, but she had neglected to provide him with the equipment for travelling by boat. Jumbo was seasick.

While the bands played and the crowd cheered, the huge creature was prodded to his feet. He was groggy and he was weak. Knees wobbling, Jumbo managed to get his seven tons in motion.

Just a few seconds before he stepped out into view, the music stopped. A hush fell over the crowd. Then Jumbo pushed his great bulk through the doors. Twelve feet high at the shoulders, fourteen feet long, seven tons of pachyderm with an eighteen-foot waistline, he literally made them gasp for breath.

Guided only by a tiny fellow named Matthew Scott, his keeper, Jumbo edged unsteadily towards the gangplank. He tested it carefully with one foot, then the other. He didn't like it.

G

His keeper whispered to him. Jumbo trumpeted and then crept out onto the gangplank. A few seconds later he was in America.

Within a matter of weeks he was in America's heart. Newspapers devoted reams of copy to describing his vastness. They told how he had been captured in the desert of Abyssinia by a tribe of Arabs, just a tiny little runt of an elephant whose mother had been drowned in a mudhole; how he had been taken to the Zoological Gardens, where he became not only the biggest elephant ever known, but the biggest attraction in the Zoo. Thousands came from all over the British Isles to marvel at his monumental proportions. Queen Victoria was a regular visitor, and she brought her grandchildren with her each visit. Winston Churchill, then a lad of tender years, had his picture taken feeding candy to Jumbo. Theodore Roosevelt spent a couple of days beside the big elephant's enclosure photographing him. Jumbo was big stuff in many ways.

It was natural that P. T. Barnum should have heard of this astounding giant and of the great crowds he attracted. Barnum knew that Jumbo would have the same failing that other male elephants acquired—that of periodic fits of violence. He waited until Jumbo was in the throes of one of these spells and sent his emissary to inquire if the Zoo would sell their chief attraction.

After long debate they decided they would part with him, but only for ten thousand dollars. Barnum paid them on the spot and figured that he was all set for a big season. And so he was, but not exactly as he anticipated. After the British newspapers had denounced the Zoo and the deal, after prominent English barristers had tried to get injunctions to prevent the transfer, after thousands of tearful families had paid their farewells to their Gargantuan chum, Jumbo took one look at the boat upon which he was to sail and baulked.

It was the biggest sitdown strike on record up to that time.

British papers ate it up. American papers were kept supplied with daily reports of Jumbo's refusal to sail, material thoughtfully supplied by Barnum's Press department.

The Zoo continued to charge admissions to see him behind his canvas wall, and they took in more than a hundred thousand dollars on this unscheduled farewell party before the ponderous pachyderm could be coaxed aboard the vessel.

The canny promoter took in three hundred thousand dollars on Jumbo the first six weeks he was in America. Barnum called him the synonym for all stupendous things, told how he had saved the life of a little girl who was attacked by a Bengal tiger. That was quite a feat for Jumbo, who had never been within a thousand miles of Bengal.

The triumphal tour continued slowly across the nation. Hundreds of thousands fought for tickets to see this wonderful creature that could actually pick apples off the wall at the twenty-six-foot mark. As a publicity stunt crippled children, blind children, and the children of local editors were given rides on his back, the highlight of their young lives.

Four years of this, and the money poured into Barnum's coffers in an endless stream.

But the pace was wearing upon the jungle giant. Jumbo had been well supplied with peanuts, apples and candy by the ton from his millions of little admirers.

Those pudgy little hands were killing him, for Jumbo's digestive system simply couldn't stand the strain. He got so that he couldn't lie down. He began to lose weight. The end of his days was in sight.

On the night of September 15, 1895, the circus was showing at St. Thomas, Ontario. Jumbo and his partner, a tiny dwarf elephant named Tom Thumb, had finished their act before the cheering thousands who packed the big tent. The elephants lumbered out the side door and started across the railroad tracks to their own cars. A gap had been left in the line of cars so they could get through, and the railroad had assured the circus men that no train was due for an hour.

Scott was guiding them along through the gap in the cars onto the tracks. Suddenly a blinding light struck them, a train whistled frantically, brakes screamed as the engineer tried to stop.

Dazzled by the light, Jumbo charged right into it. Scott leaped into a coal car; the mighty monarch of the jungle trumpeted— a thunderous blast that chilled the hearts of those in the tent; the music stopped. Then the sickening crash. Jumbo was dead of a broken neck.

The locomotive and two cars were thrown off the tracks.

Over the scene lanterns flickered through the drifting steam, and thousands stood about in awed silence. They had attended the death of a king, a beloved giant who had played his last scene to a crashing finale.

Even in death he toured the land for two years, his tremendous form stuffed and mounted on a flatcar. But he had served his time, and deserved a rest. His skeleton was presented to the American Museum of Natural History; his huge hide, mounted and well preserved, went to the Barnum Museum of Tufts College at Medford, Massachusetts. Still a symbol of stupendous things, Jumbo has been standing there ever since.

Bessler's Wonderful Wheel

SIR ISAAC NEWTON once observed, 'The seekers after perpetual motion are trying to get something from nothing.'

Of the legions who have pursued this mechanical chimera, the case of the irascible Johann Bessler and his remarkable wheel stands alone. He was either a genius without peer or he was a mountebank without equal. Johann was one or the other—but which?

Scientists of his own day were sharply divided on the question—but then they had to deal not only with his invention but with Johann himself, and that was no easy task.

Let us examine the record.

A native of Zittau, Saxony, Bessler was thirty-two years of age when he exhibited his first 'self moving wheel' at Gera in 1712. It was a wheel about three feet in diameter and four inches thick, capable (according to witnesses) of keeping itself in motion for an indefinite period without visible assistance. Once the wheel was started with a gentle push, it would accelerate to about twenty-six revolutions per minute and would maintain that speed without further assistance. Furthermore, the wheel could be geared to lift small weights by means of a rope curled round its axle.

When the learned men came to observe his creation, Bessler took the position that they were enemies *per se* and he treated them as such. Opinionated, contentious and belligerent, Bessler did not help his cause by his relations with the visitors. It is small wonder that most of them went away with their questions unanswered, mumbling that the inventor was a fraud and his wheel a fake.

The following year he brought to Leipzig another and larger version of his wheel. This second model was six feet in diameter and a foot thick, covered with heavy cloth, which was oiled and tightly stretched from rim to rim. Like its predecessor, the wheel needed but a slight push to set it in motion. Once under way, it quickly picked up speed until it reached its maximum velocity of about twenty-six turns per minute, which it could apparently maintain indefinitely unassisted. Observers agreed on one thing: as the wheel turned they could hear weights of some sort tumbling about inside it, concealed by the heavy oiled cloth stretched drum-tight from rim to rim.

The exhibition at Leipzig was successful in that the wheel performed flawlessly; otherwise, it was merely another battleground for Bessler. He soon found himself embroiled in bitter arguments with those who doubted the truth of his claims for his invention. In an effort to end these detractions once and for all, Bessler offered to exhibit his machine to a group of qualified citizens, and on October 31, 1715, a group of eleven such men witnessed the wheel in action and submitted it to certain tests of their own devising. In December they issued a report of their findings in which they unanimously concurred that '. . . the machine of Johann Bessler . . . is a true perpetual motion . . having the property to move right and left, being easily moved, but requiring great effort to stay its movement; with the power of raising . . . a box of stones 70 pounds, 8 ells high perpendicularly. . . .'

Bessler's antagonists were in no wise deterred by this declaration of the investigating body; instead, they heaped fresh ridicule on both Bessler and those who signed the report. Meanwhile the strange wheel continued to spin day and night at its accustomed rate of twenty-six revolutions per minute.

It was at this stage of his hectic career that Johann Bessler began signing his name 'Orffyreus' for some reason known only to himself. And it was also at this time (1716) that Orffyreus attracted the attention of Count Karl, Landgrave of Hesse-Cassel, one of the tiny quasi-independent states which were numerous in that stage of Germany's development. Karl had both money and prestige—Orffyreus had neither. Karl's first move was to put the eccentric inventor into a paying position as Town Councillor, a job wich gave him an income on which he could live decently and a place to call home.

It was under the patronage of Count Karl of Hesse-Cassel that Orffyreus built his last and largest wheel. He constructed the thing in a gardener's shed in the grounds of Weissenstein castle—where it could be kept under lock and key and guarded by one of the Count's men for fear that someone would see how it was built. Being suspicious even of his friends, Orffyreus kept a guard himself to guard the guard posted by the Count. The wheel was beginning to develop wheels within wheels, one might say.

A perpetual-motion wheel in our own day and age would be little more than an interesting curiosity, of course, but in the early days of the eighteenth century it assumed imposing proportions. The reason for this becomes apparent when we consider the machine in the context of its time. In those days the prime source of power was that of muscles, human or animal. Water power was being used where it was available, but it was generally undependable. The search was for some new source of power which could turn the spindles and the wheels of the little factories. The man who developed such a power source would be much in demand; if he discovered a means of extracting usable energy from a free and endless source, perpetual motion, he would be providing the answer to one of the major problems of the era.

The wondrous wheel of Orffyreus purportedly fulfilled those requirements. It could be started easily, it developed increased momentum without further assistance, and it could be used for such tasks as lifting baskets of stones without materially affecting its over-all performance. It was admittedly a promising development—if it was not a fraud, as some claimed.

The detractors of the machine were many and vociferous. There was the mathematician in Leipzig, one Claus Wagner, who had never seen the wheel and who steadfastly refused to see it. Why? Because he had calculated by his mathematical tables that such a thing was preposterous, contradictory to the laws of nature, and it could not exist—according to his figures.

Clockmakers came forward for their brief moment in the spotlight to announce that they could duplicate the performance of the wheel of Orffyreus by cleverly concealed springs and gears. Whether they could do what they claimed will never be known, for not one of the lot ever produced a single example to support his contentions.

Badgered by such characters, the difficult side of Orffyreus's character became worse, if such a thing was possible. He fought with everyone around him with the possible exception of the Count; he became so disagreeable that the guards at the room where the device was stored accepted duty there as a form of punishment.

If the machine really worked . . .

Count Karl pressed Orffyreus for an answer in the form of a demonstration which would stifle criticism once and for all; or, if it failed in that, one which would bring to an end the Count's lengthy and costly sponsorship of the device. People were beginning to wonder if Count Karl had lost his mind, and it was high time that he proved his own case as well as that of the inventor.

In October of 1717 the Count induced the inventor to transfer the new and bulkier wheel to a room in the castle of Weissenstein which was large enough to permit the device to be set up with ample space around it. This time there must be no excuse for critics to charge that the axle of the wheel touched the wall and was turned from another room by a cord.

On November 12 everything was ready. Count Karl brought in a distinguished body of investigators: Professor Gravesande of Leyden; Doctor Dietrich of Bohsen; Friedrich Hoffman, described as a famous physician and an authority on mechanics; Christian Wolff, Chancellor of the University of Halle; and John

Rowley, famed maker of mathematical instruments. There were others of less renown, all handpicked to present a broad front of talent and integrity.

They entered a large room (according to their reports) where they found a huge cloth-covered wheel sitting in the centre of the room. Their measurements determined that it was twelve feet in diameter, slightly more than fourteen inches in thickness—and it turned on an iron shaft about three-quarters of an inch in diameter. The wheel itself was described as lightly constructed of wood. Like its predecessors, Orffyreus had screened its innards by covering the space from hub to rim with tightly drawn oiled cloth.

Having determined the physical dimensions of the device, the investigators proceeded to experiment with its abilities. Baron Fisher was elected to set it in motion, which he found extremely easy. Just a push with one hand and the huge wheel began to revolve . . . slowly at first, then faster and faster, until it reached its maximum speed of twenty-six revolutions per minute.

After several experiments had been conducted, during which the wheel had supplied power to perform small tasks, the body of learned investigators carefully examined the room itself, sealing and locking every possible place of egress or entrance. Then they left the room and locked the door behind them, leaving the wheel spinning merrily at its usual rate. To make certain that the lock on the door was untouched during their absence, they sealed it with wax bearing the imprint of their several devices which they had brought for that purpose.

Fourteen days later, says the committee report, when they broke the seals and opened the door, they found the big wheel revolving just as they had left it. And again, on January 4 of 1718, they returned to the sealed room. There was the big wheel, still spinning its defiance of the accepted determinations of science.

The entire committee expressed the opinion that there was no fraud involved in the operation of the wheel. They were convinced that they had seen and tested a genuine perpetual-motion device. Writing to Sir Isaac Newton, Professor Gravesande said: '. . . I have examined these axles and am firmly persuaded that nothing from without the wheel in the least contributes to its motion.'

If it worked—as the investigators agreed that it did work— then how did it work?

Orffyreus was insanely fearful that someone would steal the secret of his remarkable wheel, cheating him of his rights. Through his friend Count Karl he offered to reveal the inner mechanism to anyone for the sum of twenty thousand pounds, that amount to be held in trust by the Count while the buyers duplicated the machine to assure themselves that they had a genuine perpetual-motion device. No one came forward with the money to take up the proposal. Knowing of the precarious state of Count Karl's finances, perhaps they did not care to entrust him with such a sum.

The silence that greeted his proposal infuriated Orffyreus. He brooded. The Count feared that he would destroy himself and had an attendant keeping close watch over his eccentric protégé. By some undisclosed piece of legerdemain the Count induced the inventor to let him see the inside of the wheel, and so far as is known, this was the only instance in which anyone other than Orffyreus ever glimpsed the workings of the device.

When the oiled cloth was stripped away, said Count Karl, he found himself gazing upon a very simple arrangement of weights and levers. Orffyreus explained that he had conceived a system whereby the weights on one side of the wheel were farther from the axle than the weights on the other side of the wheel, creating an imbalance which caused the wheel to move. The secret, if there was a secret, lay in the ingenious manner in which the weights on the ascending side of the wheel were prevented from following their normal path next to the rim. Count Karl said that these weights were blocked by small pegs which swung back out of the way as the weight passed the zenith.

The Count prudently hastened back to his quarters and wrote an account of what he had seen.

The inventor went back to his brooding. He was convinced that he had solved the classic riddle of perpetual motion, only to be spurned by those who should be rewarding him for his genius. And those investigators! Peering under the axles, placing their ears against the base to listen for concealed springs as though he, Orffyreus, had to resort to fraud. Damn them all!

Sometime during the night his mental frothings bubbled over. Orffyreus let himself into the room where his wheel was stored, and with a few blows from an axe he shattered the flimsy thing.

In that moment of unrestrained rage he seems to have shattered himself, too. Remorsefully he told the Count what he had done and promised to build another wheel as good as or better than the one he had just destroyed. But it never happened. For a few months he pottered away in his shop at the gardener's house. He quarrelled with the Count. And when the wreckage of his wheel was destroyed by fire, the inventor and his patron reached a parting of the ways. Orffyreus became an embittered wanderer who died in November of 1745.

Did he really have a perpetual-motion machine?

On the basis of Count Karl's description of what he saw, it seems that Johann Bessler's creation was merely another example of the unbalanced wheel, one of the oldest of all methods by which ingenious fellows have sought to attain perpetual motion. Scientists say they can explain why the unbalanced wheel cannot turn itself. Let us remember that these same scientists can also prove that a bumble bee cannot fly.

And what could be more exasperating to orthodox science than the spectacle of a bumble bee flying around the ever-spinning wheel of Johann Bessler?

Brig of Doom

WHY would a ship's crew desert the vessel when there was no storm and the ship was sound and full of valuable cargo?

If you can answer that question, you can solve the riddle of the *Marie Celeste*, a mystery which has defied the experts for more than eighty years.

When the *Marie Celeste* was found drifting and deserted by the British ship *Dei Gratia* about 300 miles off the coast of Portugal on the afternoon of December 4th, 1872, she touched off a chain reaction of controversy that reached a high point of silliness in 1922 when one frustrated 'expert', D. G. Ball, wrote in *Nautical Magazine* that 'the *Marie Celeste* had never existed in the first place'! Unfortunately for the neatness of his hypothesis it does not square with the recorded facts: a fatal shortcoming in this instance.

The court records at Gibraltar alone are sufficient to prove that the *Marie Celeste* did exist and by the strange nature of her existence carved a niche for herself in the annals of the sea.

The *Dei Gratia* was moving along briskly before a fair breeze when Mate Oliver Deveau spotted a smaller ship labouring slowly on a path which would intercept that of his own vessel. The newcomer's sails were furled for the most part, she was short-sailed, as the mate reported to Captain Morehouse. The *Dei Gratia* 'spoke' the other craft, but there was no response to the mate's calls through the long brass trumpet. Captain Morehouse put about and came up alongside the *Marie Celeste*.

Strange that there should be no one on deck! The wheel was untended, there was no sign of life. Deveau and three seamen crossed over and boarded the brig.

In their subsequent testimony before the British court at Gibraltar the members of that boarding party agreed on what they had found: No one on board; more than three feet of water in the hold; lazarette and fore hatches both open; binnacle compass shattered; the skylight of the captain's cabin open.

Mate Deveau told the court: 'The captain's clothing was all in proper place and even the log book was on the mate's desk in his cabin. There seemed to be everything left behind in the cabin as if left in a hurry, but everything in its place. I noticed the impression in the captain's bed as of a child having lain there.'

The boarding party found 1,700 barrels of alcohol in the hold of the *Marie Celeste*, a rich haul for the ship that could tow her into port for salvage. Captain Morehouse ordered Mate Deveau to take his skeleton crew and run the derelict into port at Gibraltar, to register their find and claim the salvage rights. Deveau did as he was told, but he ran into trouble from the moment he touched shore at Gibraltar, nine days after he pulled away from the *Dei Gratia*. The Marshal of the Vice-Admiralty considered the size and value of the *Marie Celeste's* cargo and decided that no one in his right mind would desert seventy-five thousand dollars' worth of alcohol in mid-ocean without visible reason. Therefore it had to be piracy. When Captain Morehouse made port a few days later he found his prize crew in prison, awaiting trial like common buccaneers.

The court had to prove its case, of course, so its first move was to search the *Marie Celeste* for evidence of foul play. Under the berth of the missing captain a battered old Italian officer's sword was found—and stained suspiciously, too. A doctor was appointed by the court to determine the nature of the stains. After due consideration the good Dr. Patron reported that the stains on the sword, like the stains of the deck, were not blood.

Had the ship's crew panicked when it had struck something, a reef perhaps? The court employed a diver who carefully examined the bottom of the mysterious brig. No trace of any injury—no sign that the *Marie Celeste* had bumped into anything that had in any way scarred her sturdy hull. She was as sound as she was baffling.

Why, then, had Captain Briggs, his wife, his little daughter and the nine crew members of the *Marie Celeste* deserted her suddenly in mid-ocean? Had the alcohol leaked fumes in such quantity that the captain ordered the abandonment in order to get away before fire and explosion killed all of them? Had the crew tapped the alcohol and, when discovered, murdered the captain and his family and, in a drunken frenzy, then abandoned the ship, only to perish in their efforts to escape?

Or, as sailors whispered among themselves, was the *Marie Celeste* merely another jinx ship, foredoomed to bring sorrow to all who dealt with her?

Let's look at the record.

This enigmatic brig which was brought to port by the prize crew of the *Dei Gratia* had not always been the *Marie Celeste*. She had been christened the *Amazon* when she was built back in 1861 and her first skipper, Captain Robert McClellan, took sick aboard her on her maiden voyage and died a few days later. Her second skipper, John Parker, found ill fortune dogging his footsteps. He made no money for the owners and soon found himself jobless. His successor piled the brig up on the rocky Cape Breton Island, bankrupting the owners. John Beatty bought her cheaply and lost her quickly. For she went right out and knocked her bottom out on a rocky reef along the Maine coast.

In November of 1868 she was sold as a condemned hulk to Richard Haines of New York, who sought to give her a new lease of life by changing her name to *Marie Celeste*. Haines went bankrupt in ten months and the *Marie Celeste* went to James Winchester, who was fighting a court action charging him with fraudulent ownership at the time the ship set out on the trip that was to launch her name indelibly in the annals of maritime mysteries.

As the brig touched briefly at Staten Island on that memorable voyage, the captain's wife penned a quick note to her mother. Dated November 7, 1872, it says in part: 'Benjie [Capt. Briggs] thinks we have a pretty peaceable set [the crew] this time if they continue as they have begun.' Then she adds ominously—'Can't tell yet how smart they are.'

Mrs. Briggs posted her letter and the brig slipped out into the trackless wastes of the Atlantic for her strange rendezvous with fate.

The dramatic discovery of the abandoned vessel in December of 1872 did not mark a turning point in her hectic career. The evil reputation she had acquired clung to her more tenaciously than ever. When the court at Gibraltar ordered her returned to her owners, a Captain Blatchford came from Massachusetts to run her on to Italy to discharge her cargo of alcohol. Back in Boston several prospective purchasers showed up, but once they learned her story they lost interest.

By this time her owner, Mr. Winchester, had had more than his fill of this ill-starred brig. He managed to sell her to a Captain David Cartwright, losing slightly more than eight thousand dollars in the process.

Captain Cartwright loaded her with lumber for Montevideo. She got there, but in the stormy trip she had lost all her rigging and all the lumber that had been stored on her deck. Her skipper found an unsuspecting soul who wanted a load of horses delivered up the coast. The horses died en route, and the skipper himself had to be put ashore at St. Helena, where he passed away. Cartwright was glad to dispose of his jinx ship to a schemer named Wesley Gove.

Mr. Gove was a man with a plan. He did not propose to trust to the vagaries of commerce for making a profit. Like many schemers both before and since his time, this precious conniver intended to beat the insurance companies.

He needed a skipper who was amenable to such work, for a price, of course, and in Captain Gilman Parker he found his man. Gove took out cargo insurance for twenty-five thousand dollars;

Parker loaded the *Marie Celeste* with furniture and cloth for Haiti.

A few miles from their destination the skipper passed out grog to all hands. Roaring drunk himself, he pointed to a reef on which the waves were crashing and ordered the helmsman to ram her head-on. With a crash the *Marie Celeste* struck the sharp coral; gutted, she began to settle. The crew took another drink to their handiwork and pulled for the shore.

Gove and Parker found themselves hauled into court on a charge of barratry, and, confronted with the testimony of the crew, they knew they faced conviction. But before they could be brought to trial Parker died, his mate died, and all six of the insurance companies involved had gone bankrupt!

Gove went free for lack of prosecution.

And what became of Captain Briggs, his wife and daughter and the nine sailors?

Like many another riddle of the sea, time has closed the books on the *Marie Celeste* and our question must go unanswered.

From Nags to Riches

In the dear, dead days before the motor car became the ruler of the roads, Chicago had a special officer known as the knacker. His job, or privilege, was seeing that all the horses that died or were killed on the city streets were promptly hauled away to the glue factory. There he sold the animal, which had cost him nothing, and pocketed the clear profit.

One of the smartest knackers Chicago ever had was a lad named Jack Brennock. He started his political career by getting appointed to the fire department. But Jack had a yen for more money and easier money What could be simpler than picking up dead horses for free and selling them? Up to that time the firemen had simply notified the glue companies and permitted them to come and get the animal. Jack soon corrected that economic error. He paid the firemen a buck for the tip and sold the horse for five dollars. Besides, Brennock was the only man in Chicago legally permitted to remove dead horses from the streets. No chance of any new connivers sneaking into his playground later on. It was a wonderful way of getting rich. Within a year Jack no longer did the actual work. He had progressed to the point where ten wagon crews took care of that. All Jack did was to keep the politicians happy and count his proceeds. He amassed wealth so rapidly that within ten years he was a millionaire living in a palatial estate on the exclusive west side of Chicago.

Up to the advent of Jack Brennock, a special routine had been observed among fire horses who shuffled off the mortal coils. The city had permitted their buddies at the fire stations to handle their equine friends, giving them funerals in some city property well out of town. But Brennock laughed at such business. Funerals for horses? Nothing doing! They were grist for his mill, and profits for his bank accounts. His former buddies in the fire department could stand it no longer. One of the longtime favourites, old Danny Boy, made his last run on a bitter wintry day. He slipped on an icy corner and broke his leg. Old Bill Hannon had to climb off the wagon and shoot him. And Brennock's men came up in force and took him away to the common fate, the glue factory. The firemen were outraged. They got together and put the Connacht curse on Jack Brennock for his high-handed treatment of old comrades.

Mr. Brennock was becoming bored with life. His fabulous enterprise was providing more money than he could spend in normal pursuits, so he took up horse racing. He bought a fine string of colts, built magnificent stables for them, and hired the inevitable expensive retinue of handlers and trainers.

By all the laws of horse racing he should have had some success, but fate had decreed otherwise. Brennock had reckoned without the Connacht curse. In spite of all the money he spent, millions of dollars, in spite of ten years of racing and heavy betting, Brennock never had one single winner.

One day the banker called him in and gave him the bad news. He was right back where he had started twenty years before, broke. But now he was getting along in years and he no longer had the lucrative concession that had made him rich.

Jack Brennock ended his days as a janitor in a shabby walk-up apartment and they found him dead one morning in the street, like one of the nags who had brought him a fortune. His was the strange case of a man who made millions of dollars on dead horses and lost every cent of it on live ones.

A Dream Full of Headlines

EDWARD SAMSON was listed as a news editor of the Boston *Globe* in August of 1883, but the pay was not commensurate with the title. He drew the meagre salary of a reporter and that was hardly enough to cover his living costs even in those days.

Samson had been having a few with the boys; indeed, he may have had a few too many before he showed up at the *Globe* to sleep it off on a tattered couch in the artist's office. Shortly after three o'clock in the morning, after seven hours on the couch, Samson got to his feet and tried to clear his mind of the terrible dream he had been experiencing. Drenched with perspiration, he hung his shirt over the back of a chair beside an open window, doused his head with a pitcher of water and sat down to think, if possible.

What a dream it had been! Thank God it hadn't been real—the screams of those doomed mortals were still ringing in his ears. Never before had he experienced such clarity of detail—it was as if he had been watching the tragedy unfold by observing it from a grandstand seat on the topmast of a ship, a seat that was strangely exempt from the menace that spread before him.

Samson sat there in the deserted office for a few minutes trying to decide what to do next. Thanks to a lucky hunch, he lit a candle and began to write out his dream in longhand.

He described in detail how thousands of fear-maddened

natives on the island of Pralape, near Java, had fled towards the sea to escape a stream of seething lava that gushed from the volcano behind them.

They found themselves trapped between the red-hot lava and the boiling sea. He wrote of other thousands driven into the water by rivers of flowing mud fifty feet high, of thunderous cannonading that jarred heaven and earth, of ships that were rolled over by giant waves—and finally, as a fitting climax to this cataclysm, a tremendous explosion that destroyed the island of Pralape in its entirety, with only a fire-spouting crater in the foaming sea to mark its passing.

Samson scrawled 'Important' across his story and left it lying on the desk.

There the editor found it when he came in the next morning. Naturally he assumed that it was something that Samson had taken off the wire during the night, and he ran it with an eight-column banner headline. Other papers heard of his scoop and wanted details. The editor fed the story to the telegraph which connected him with New York. There, it went on the Associated Press wires to the nation, and scores of leading dailies in Chicago, Cincinnati, Cleveland, San Francisco and elsewhere front-paged this story of a catastrophe of unprecedented proportions without realizing that it was based on nothing more substantial than a reporter's night mare. It was the big story on August 29, 1883.

Then reaction set in. There was no follow-up to the story for two very good reasons: first, the lack of communications with the remote part of the world where the thing supposedly happened; second, the newsman who wrote the story in the first place couldn't dream up the sequel to it. Dead end.

The publisher of the Boston *Globe* demanded an explanation, and Samson shamefacedly admitted the truth. He had committed the unpardonable sin of turning in a story which could not be substantiated in any way, for there was no record of any such island as Pralape in the Boston library. Samson's lame explanation that he had not intended the story for publication was wasted effort—the thing had already been published.

There was hell to pay, of course. Scores of embarrassed newspapers were confronted with the necessity of going before their readers and admitting that they had been victims of a hoax. Samson was promptly fired, of course, but that did not solve the problem for the papers. They waited for the Associated Press to lead them out of the morass. The Boston *Globe* made ready a retraction and prepared to become the laughing stock of their competitors who had been 'scooped' on the great catastrophe.

Then Nature went to work. Unusually high waves began running ashore on the west coast of the United States. From scattered points came fragmentary reports that something very unusual had taken place in the Indian Ocean. Tidal waves had surged over thousands of communities in Malaya and India. Loss of life was heavy but undetermined. The newspapers printed what they could get and withheld their statements of apology for the hoax.

Within a few days there could no longer be any doubt that a stupendous cataclysm had occurred. From Australia came reports that the air had vibrated with the sound of heavy aerial cannonading to the north; great swells rolled against the west coast of the United States, Mexico and South America. It circled the world—the greatest sea wave ever recorded. Ships limped into port around the Indian Ocean to report that the volcano of Krakatoa had exploded in the Straits of Sunda, obliterating the island and its thousands of inhabitants in one globe-shaking blast that produced barometric oscillation which was recorded all over the world, an atmospheric wave that circled the earth three times.

It was one of the great news stories of all time, and the papers made the most of it—especially those papers which had carried Ed Samson's dream article on the explosion of Pralape. The explosion of Krakatoa literally was world-shaking, the mightiest convulsion of Nature ever recorded in history.

As the details of the story unfolded, the Boston *Globe* tossed its retraction in the waste basket and ran Samson's picture on page one. They took the position that they had known it all the time, although they were understandably vague about the source of their scoop. Krakatoa was in the headlines of the world, and Samson was back on the payroll of the *Globe*, devoting his attention to daily coverage of the great event.

Krakatoa began writhing and roaring on August 27th, 1883, blew itself to bits on the following day, and sank beneath the boiling waters of Sunda Straits on the morning of the 29th. In other words, the vivid and terrifying events which Ed Samson was dreaming about were actually taking place at that same instant half way around the earth from where he lay tossing on the couch in the office of the Boston *Globe*. His description of the nightmare had closely paralleled the event itself, with one important exception. Ed had, for some reason which he could not explain, identified the doomed island as Pralape, whereas it was actually Krakatoa that was destroyed.

Edward Samson was old and nearly blind when the last paragraph of his remarkable experience was written. The Dutch Historical Society remembered his story and as a memento they sent him an old map which listed Krakatoa by its native name— Pralape—a name which had not been used for almost a hundred and fifty years.

In the annals of journalism, Ed Samson's dream of the disaster at Krakatoa is probably strangest of all.

The Disappearance of Oliver Larch

Is it possible for a human being to walk off the earth?

Science says that it is not, but if that is correct, then what happened to Oliver Larch?

Christmas Eve of 1889 found the countryside around South Bend, Indiana, covered with several inches of soft snow. A few miles out of the city, at the farm where Oliver Larch lived with his parents, an old-fashioned Christmas party was under way.

The family minister and his wife were there, along with a circuit judge from South Bend and an attorney from Chicago who had long been a friend of the family. After dinner they all retired to the parlour for conversation and for singing to the accompaniment of the old-style pump organ which Mrs. Larch played quite well, having been church organist for many years.

It was a delightful get-together which had become an annual event for this little group. The attorney from Chicago had lost his wife a few years before, and she was buried in the country churchyard a mile or so from the Larch home. The minister had been a schoolmate of Mr. Larch. Everybody knew each other well, and they made a very congenial group, reminiscing, laughing, singing, and eating the popcorn which eleven-year-old Oliver Larch was popping on the big kitchen range.

Outside, the snow had stopped falling. It was about five or six inches deep, a soft, fluffy blanket that lay as it fell, for there was no breeze on this black, starless night.

A few minutes before eleven o'clock, Oliver's father noticed that the grey granite bucket which held the drinking-water needed filling. He asked Oliver to run out to the well and bring in a bucket of fresh water. Oliver slipped on a pair of overshoes and went out the side door as his father went back into the parlour to be with the guests.

About ten seconds after Oliver closed the door behind him the adults in the front room heard him scream for help. They ran out the same door Oliver had used. Mr. Larch brought a kerosene lamp which sent its flickering yellow rays out over the snow for a few feet. Scream after scream chilled the little gathering.

'Help! Help! They've got me! Help! Help! Help!'

The witnesses afterwards agreed that the cries for help were coming from overhead. Somewhere up there in the stygian blackness Oliver Larch was in mortal fear, his screams growing fainter and fainter until they finally became inaudible.

By the light of the lamp the men made out Oliver's footprints in the snow. He had gone about half way to the well, which was about seventy-five feet from the house across the open yard, when his tracks ended abruptly. The grey granite bucket lay on its side in the snow about fifteen feet away on the left side of Oliver's track. There were no other marks of any kind in the soft snow. Just Oliver's footprints . . . and the bucket . . . and silence.

Subsequently, investigation confirmed the testimony of those who were present on that fateful Christmas Eve. Oliver Larch never reached the well. He never turned aside in the snow, for there were no other marks than his own footprints which extended a little more than thirty feet from the side porch before they came to a termination. Reluctantly, investigators were forced to the conclusion that Oliver Larch had gone . . . upwards!

The cries fading away in the blackness overhead had been no illusion after all. It was the only explanation for his sudden and dramatic disappearance. And assuming that he had gone up into the night, the next question was—how?

The boy weighed about seventy-five pounds, far too much for an eagle to lift—far beyond the capabilities of two eagles, for that matter.

'Help! Help! They've got me!' he had screamed.

They? Not eagles certainly.

A balloon, perhaps? Official records show that there were no balloons aloft anywhere in the country on that wintry night. Airplanes were many years in the future.

Because it defied logical explanation, the disappearance of this boy was quietly filed away and forgotten.

The mystery of Oliver Larch is as baffling today as it was on that Christmas Eve of 1889 when he walked out the side door of his home and vanished as completely as if he had literally walked off the earth.

Three Smart Dogs

SEDALIA'S SENSATIONAL SETTER

JIM was an English setter. His death in Sedalia, Missouri, at the age of twelve brought to a close one of the most incredible canine careers on record, a performance that compares favourably with any documented cases.

The dog was about four years old when his owner, Sam Van Arsdale, a hotel owner, discovered his unique abilities. He discovered that if he spoke the name of certain trees on the hotel lawn, Jim would go at once to the tree that was named and place his paw on it. Furthermore, the dog demonstrated that he could identify about ten different makes of automobiles and could find specific licence numbers.

His reputation spread rapidly when word got around that the dog was also capable of predicting winning horses. Van Arsdale would write the names of the entrants in the Kentucky Derby on slips of paper, place them before Jim, and ask the setter to name the winner. Witnesses, including several prominent citizens of Sedalia, reported that Jim unerringly put his paw on the slips that bore the names of the eventual winners of six consecutive Derbys. Van Arsdale, no gambler himself, did not bet on the tips and would not permit the witnesses to profit by the dog's predictions. A movie company offered a contract for more than a quarter of a million dollars to the fabulous setter, only to have its proposal rejected.

The dog's uncanny performance began in 1929, and within five years he was being subjected to tests by various scientific groups, including Professors Durant and Dickinson from the University of Missouri. They conducted a public experiment at Columbia, Missouri, at which an estimated nine hundred persons were present. The professors gave instructions to the dog in several languages—Spanish, Italian, and German, among others—and the dog followed instructions without error. He was told to go into the crowd and pick out a woman with a blue dress and white hat, a man with a black moustache, a child with long, light hair, an elm tree, a sycamore—and Jim found all of them, promptly and correctly.

He was invited to appear before the Missouri state legislature, and again he displayed his remarkable ability to carry out instructions. This time, a telegraphist tapped out orders in code—dots and dashes—and as the names of certain members of the legislature were spelled out, Jim hurried away from the speaker's stand to the person he had been ordered to find.

In 1936 Jim's eyesight was failing, and he showed less and less interest in the matters for which he was famous. But 1936 was election year and interest in the outcome was keen, so perhaps it was inevitable that Jim's prediction should be sought. When the dog named Roosevelt as the winner there was considerable speculation that the poor old fellow had become senile. Hadn't the famed *Literary Digest* poll predicted a landslide for Landon?

Jim was right again, of course. When he died in 1937 the President was again Franklin D. Roosevelt, just as he had predicted.

ROLF—THE 'TALKING DOG' OF MANNHEIM

The summer of 1913 was a busy one for Professors Schoeller and Ziegler of the University of Berlin. Not only did they spend two months with the horses of Elberfeld—they also spent some weeks with a most unusual dog named Rolf, the property of Mrs. Paula Moekel, of Mannheim.

Rolf is sometimes described as a Bedlington terrier, at other times as being of doubtful ancestry. Be that as it may, he exhibited signs of intelligence which have seldom been duplicated in the canine world. And according to his owner, he started the whole business by injecting himself into a little family conversation. Mrs. Moekel was mildly reproving her young daughter for making a mistake in adding some figures. Jokingly she said to the child, 'Why, I believe that Rolf could do that little problem without a mistake!' Then, said Mrs. Moekel, she turned to Rolf and asked him if he knew what two and two amounted to. To her surprise, and to that of her family, the dog came to her and promptly tapped his paw on her arm four times. She put other simple problems to him with similar results until the dog finally tired of it and walked away for a nap, leaving his owner and her family speechless with amazement.

Gradually, Mrs. Moekel says, she worked out an alphabet which Rolf could use. Like that of the Elberfeld horses it consisted of taps for various letters and numerals. Unlike that of the horses, it did not include every letter of the alphabet, for the dog either could not or would not use V, Q, Z or X. Unfortunately for both dog and owner, they never worked out a simplified code for the alphabet, and it was a laborious procedure for the dog to tap out letters requiring as many as twenty taps for a single letter.

When Drs. Schoeller and Ziegler tested Rolf they reported that they found him capable of doing simple addition and subtraction with some multiplication of small numbers of not more than two figures. He could read and write with approximately the ability of an intelligent ten-year-old child. His spelling, the doctors reported, was simplified and phoneticized to the utmost. He could seek and find words to define an object or picture placed before him. For instance, Dr. Ziegler placed before him a bouquet in a vase and asked the dog what it was. Rolf seemed puzzled for a moment, then he laboriously tapped out, 'Glass with little flowers.'

Drs. Ziegler and Schoeller also found that Rolf could distinguish colours, could count money, and that he could separate marks from pfennigs.

In the course of some tests conducted by Professor William Mackenzie of the University of Genoa, the savant was endeavouring to determine how many words the dog could identify. One of the test words was *Herbst*, meaning autumn. Could Rolf tell what it meant?

The dog reportedly tapped out, 'Time for apples.'

Also to Professor Mackenzie, who had shown him a card marked with red and blue squares, Rolf replied, 'Blue, red, lots of cubes.' Another learned man who visited the famed 'talking dog' of Mannheim was Monsieur Edmond Duchatel, vice-president of the Societé Universelle d'Etudes Psychiques of Paris, whose report confirms all that Schoeller, Mackenzie and Ziegler had experienced, with the addition of one incident which occurred during a session at which Dr. Duchatel's secretary was present. The secretary, a prissy middle-aged lady, was invited to put a question to the dog.

She inquired, 'Is there anything you would like me to do for you?'

Rolf replied, *'Wedeln'*—in other words, 'Wag your tail!'

CHRIS—THE CANINE PRODIGY

Dr. Henry Nugent, professor of educational psychology at Rhode Island College of Education, calls him 'a living riddle, enthusiastic but baffling'.

Investigators representing Dr. J. B. Rhine, famed parapsychologist of Duke University, call Chris 'an amazing fellow who defies explanation'.

His owners, Mr. and Mrs. George H. Wood of East Greenwich, Rhode Island, just call him Chris. They do not try to explain him, which undoubtedly saves them a great deal of time and trouble. Chris is part beagle, part accident. He is a friendly little fellow who shares the Wood home with two big cats. Most of the time he is all dog, chasing cars, running rabbits, getting into fights. But when called upon to do so, Chris can assume the mantle of respectability long enough to present curious scientists with fresh reasons for pondering the limitations of man's knowledge.

According to Chris's owner, the whole thing began in 1953 when a visiting friend happened to mention that he had been able to teach his dog to count up to ten. Could Chris be taught to duplicate that feat? Mr. Wood thought it would be fun to find out, so he began showing Chris how to count by tapping with his paws on the arm of the chair. In a matter of a few weeks Wood discovered that Chris was not only learning, but was apparently waiting for Wood to catch up with him. After teaching him addition and subtraction up to one hundred, Mr. Wood suddenly discovered that Chris could count up to a million. There was a similar educational sprint when Chris took up square root, and his amazed master found that the dog could do cube root problems as well—in fact, that the dog showed unmistakable evidence of knowing the mathematical scale from beginning to end.

Did he know anything beyond that? Mr. Wood told newsmen that he and his wife wrote the letters of the alphabet on a card and put it on the floor. They explained to Chris, he says, that each letter was to be given a number, so that the dog could spell words by tapping out the correct number of times with his paw. After five minutes of gazing at the card and at his owners, the card was picked up and there was never any occasion to refer to it again. That was in October of 1954, and in the ensuing time Chris has tapped out thousands of replies to questions, using the code he scanned so briefly on that one occasion.

Since the discovery that Chris could and would tap out answers to questions, he has been called upon to do so more than fifty thousand times. His owners make no charge for this, nor will they accept any gratuities. Naturally they have had their share of critics who have watched the dog at work and then denounced him as a fraud or a satanic monster who should be destroyed.

In addition to the university representatives from Rhode

Island and Duke, Chris has been tested by such visitors as two research specialists from Dupont. They concocted on the spur of the moment a complicated mathematical problem of the type that is customarily fed into electronic calculators. Instead of tapping out the answer almost instantaneously, as usual, this poser took Chris four minutes to solve. The researchers who had proposed it needed ten minutes to arrive at the same answer Chris had produced in four.

How does he do it? Chris replies, 'Smart dog.'

Investigators have found no reason to disagree with him.

Claimed by Fire

MAN'S first experience with chemical reaction undoubtedly involved the use of fire. Through countless ages he learned to use it to his advantage and finally to tame it to help him do his work. But it still serves notice from time to time that man has not mastered it, and that it has secrets still withheld from him.

Sometimes fire plays ghastly pranks which make headlines before they are filed away among the unexplained. For instance:

On the morning of Monday, July 2, 1951, Mrs. P. M. Carpenter of 1200 Cherry Street, Northeast, St. Petersburg, Florida, went to the door of the room occupied by Mrs. Mary H. Reeser, 67, whom she had last seen the night before. When Mrs. Carpenter went to Mrs. Reeser's room it was a few minutes past eight o'clock, and it was time for their morning coffee. She also had a telegram which the Western Union boy had been unable to deliver, because Mrs. Reeser did not answer his knock.

Mrs. Carpenter found that the doorknob to her tenant's room was so hot that she could not grip it. Alarmed, she ran outside and called for help. Some house painters working near by hurried over and forced the door to Mrs. Reeser's room.

The apartment was unbearably hot. The windows were open. Near one of these open windows were the charred remains of an armchair and the equally charred remains of Mary Reeser. There was little left of either.

Subsequent investigation by detectives, chemists and pathologists developed some very strange information, much of which does not coincide with man's understanding of fire.

Mrs. Reeser had last been seen alive about nine o'clock the preceding night by her son, Dr. Richard Reeser, and her landlady and friend, Mrs. P. M. Carpenter. She was last seen sitting in the easy chair where she died, wearing a rayon nightgown, cloth bedroom slippers and a light housecoat.

When the landlady and the painters forced their way into the room next day, Mrs. Reeser's one hundred and seventy pounds had been reduced to less than ten pounds of charred material by a fierce heat which had destroyed all of her except her skull, a few vertebrae and her left foot, which was virtually unchanged by the heat. The chair on which she had been sitting was completely burned up, only the coil springs remaining.

The room in which she died in this odd inferno was strangely exempt from the effects of the heat. Above a line about four feet from the floor there was a thick sooty deposit on walls and curtains. A mirror on the wall had cracked from the heat. Window screens were thickly packed with soot. The armchair, a near-by floor lamp and a small end table were destroyed. Beneath the chair there was a burned spot on the rug. As mute testimony to the terrific heat were the remains of two paraffin candles on a small dressing-table about twelve feet from the charred armchair. The candles had melted and dripped off the edge of the dressing-table, leaving the uncharred wicks stretched limply across the holders. The effects of heat were numerous and plain above the four-foot line, but below that point the fire had left no marks.

Investigation disclosed that the fire had melted a wall outlet into which the floor lamp and an electric clock were plugged, blowing a fuse which had stopped the clock at twenty past four. The small wall-type gas heater was turned off.

The strange death of Mary Reeser left the authorities baffled. Edward Davies, arson specialist for the National Board of Underwriters, was brought up from Tampa to probe the case. He said, 'We do not know that it was a fire—we just don't know what could have caused it.'

His bewilderment was not unmatched. Professor Wilton Korgmann of the University of Pennsylvania Graduate School of Medicine admitted that he, too, was baffled and amazed.

'Never have I seen a human skull shrunk by intense heat as Mrs. Reeser's was shrunk,' said Professor Korgmann. 'The opposite is always true. The skulls have either been abnormally swollen or have virtually exploded into hundreds of pieces. It is the most amazing thing I have ever seen.'

Had the unfortunate Mrs. Reeser been struck by lightning?

The Weather Bureau reported no lightning that night in the St. Petersburg area.

Had she fallen asleep with a cigarette in her hand and burned to death through ignition of her clothing?

Experts agreed that it would have required a temperature of twenty-five hundred to three thousand degrees for hours to produce the cremation effect which Mary Reeser had undergone. Burning clothing was inadequate as an explanation; the electricity was off because the fire had shorted the line and blown the fuse; the gas heater was also turned off.

The F.B.I. made an analysis of the body ashes in this case and reported that there was no indication that any fluids or chemicals had been used to induce burning.

The baffled St. Petersburg authorities felt constrained to close the case with some sort of statement other than one officially admitting that they could not solve the mystery. The Chief of Police, J. R. Reichart, and Cass Burgess, Chief of Detectives, jointly signed a statement in which they attributed the armchair cremation of Mary Reeser to falling asleep with a cigarette in her hand and dying as the result of being cremated by the burning of her own body fat.

Exactly what did cause her strange death may never be known; and the cigarette-burning-clothing theory, inadequate by known principles involved, is clearly nothing more than a convenient hypothesis. If the various scientists and laboratories which analysed the case could not solve it, then certainly there is no reason to expect more of two police officers, willing and sincere though they undoubtedly were.

The fiery death which came to Mrs. Mary Reeser was by no means unprecedented in the annals of necroscopy. In the *Hampshire* (Eng.) *Advertiser* for March 4, 1905, there is a report on the fate which befell aged Andrew Kiley and his wife during the night of February 26th or on the morning of the following day. This couple lived in a stone cottage at Butlock Heath, near Southampton. On the morning of the 26th passers-by heard what they described as scratchings and mutterings from the cottage. Officials were called and they had to break the latch in order to gain entrance. They found Mr. Kiley burned to death on the floor, his body almost entirely consumed by a fire that had only scorched the rug beneath him. His wife, an invalid, had been burned to death in the big chair where she sat, about twelve feet from her husband. She was charred but recognizable according to witnesses.

What burned these two oldsters to death without destroying the house? The officials could not imagine, and they had little time to investigate, for the house itself burned down that night.

The *New York Herald* for December 27, 1916, reports the case of Lillian Green, employed as housekeeper for the Lake Denmark Hotel, a resort located about seven miles from Dover, New Jersey.

The proprietor of the hotel, Tom Morphey, was awakened by sounds of moaning which had aroused his pet dog. Unable to quiet the animal, Morphey got up and began a search for the source of the moans. He found the housekeeper, Miss Green, burned and dying on the floor of her room. On the floor beneath her was a small charred spot; her clothing was entirely consumed. She died without being able to tell what had happened, or why. Authorities were at a loss to understand how a fire of intensity sufficient to do such damage to the victim and her clothing did almost nothing to the rug on which she lay.

The *New York Sun* for January 24, 1930, reports on an even more baffling case. Mrs. Stanley Lake of Kingston, New York, had burned to death under strange circumstances and the coroner's jury, after pronouncing it accidental from unknown causes, added this comment: 'Although her body was severely burned, her clothing was not even scorched.'

The Secret Power of Cheiro the Great

THE body of an elderly man was sprawled on the floor in front of the fireplace. The room, like the body, was quite cold. It was clear to the representatives of Scotland Yard that the victim had been murdered by liberal application of the andirons. On the question of who used the weapon, however, they were completely in the dark.

Robbery could not be ruled out as a possible motive, though there was little in the shabby elegance of the quarters to indicate any wealth worthy of the name. The suddenly deceased was not known to be a quarrelsome man, and he had no known enemies.

Scotland Yard was stumped.

An impeccably attired young man presented himself at the door just as the detectives were preparing to leave. Could he be of service? Well, you never know in such cases, and it's always best not to overlook any possibilities. While the body was being removed, detectives led the young man into the room where the deed had been done. He glanced around casually, asking if he might examine one of the many bloody handprints which marked the walls.

Head in hand, for a moment he gazed at one of the handprints.

'The murderer is a young man, gentlemen. He is well-to-do, he carries a small gold watch in his left front trouser pocket . . . and he is a near relative of the gentleman whose body was just taken from this room.'

The Scotland Yard boys were ready to toss this smug fop out on his ear for wasting their time with such nonsense. But there were a couple of correspondents for the London papers on hand and they smelled a story. Who was this fancy dresser who presumed to deduce so much from a bloody handprint on a grimy wall?

'Cheiro—Cheiro the Great!' he told them, as he handed them his lavishly embossed business cards.

The story made the papers on Monday. On the following day the extraordinary palmist was back in headlines, for the police had found their man. The murderer was not only young and well-to-do, with his gold watch in his left front trouser pocket, but he was also the son of the man who was murdered—the near relative Cheiro had foretold.

In a matter of weeks Cheiro became the rage of London. He basked in the adulation that came his way, and he banked sizable sums regularly, his fees for counselling his clients on their futures.

Cheiro left England in 1893 for New York, where he fitted himself out with a lavish suite of offices on Park Avenue. Here again success came easily for him. As business began to pour into the offices of the fabulous fortune-teller the Press inevitably became interested in the man and his methods. A young lady from the *New York World* called to inquire whether he would be willing to submit to a series of tests which the paper had in mind. The request was actually little more than a veiled threat of exposure —if he refused or if he failed.

He accepted the challenge without a moment's hesitation.

The *World* publicized the event widely. They were to submit to this fantastic fellow thirteen palm-prints of New York citizens. These prints would have no identifying marks of any kind, and from them Cheiro was to tell what he could about each person—if he could indeed tell anything at all.

If the paper thought to scuttle him by this procedure, they

reckoned without their man. At the hour for the test a committee of well-known citizens was on hand to act as judges. The thirteen palm-prints were laid out on a table, face up. Cheiro was invited to work his magic—or whatever it was that he used.

He spent little time with the first print he picked up, merely glancing at it for a second or two and tossing it back on the table.

'Gentlemen,' he said, 'that is the print of an Irishman. He once did hard labour, but he is now rich and powerful.'

A ripple of comment ran through the judging committee. The print to which Cheiro referred had been made by Richard Croker, an Irish immigrant who had worked his way from hod-carrier to head of Tammany Hall.

But Cheiro had not finished with the print.

'Furthermore, gentlemen, the Irishman who made that print was once a wrestler. In my opinion he is also a very effective speaker with a flair for politics.'

Score one on each count for the palmist.

Cheiro picked up another print from the table, glanced at it and tossed it back beside the first.

'This fellow had a brush with genius, although he is not quite a genius. He merits greater honours than he will receive in life.'

The second print was that of Reginald De Koven, composer of the operetta *Robin Hood*—a work which he never quite equalled again.

Without hesitation Cheiro ran through the prints the committee had provided as his test. Without failure he identified each and every one, including that of a woman whom he described as a child of fate with great talent and ambition—but with great unhappiness as well. It was that of Lillian Russell.

Less than ten minutes after he began, Cheiro had disposed of all the prints except one; that one he had picked up several times and each time he had frowned as he replaced it on the table without comment.

Now only this print remained. Why had he failed to deal with it before? Was it because he could not? Was this the print that was to trip him up in public—to show that he could not read the story from *every* palm-print, as he claimed? The members of the committee were on the edge of their chairs; there was a feeling of tension as Cheiro turned his back on the table and dabbed a handkerchief to his brow. Was he going to pass this last print? Why?

It seems likely that this strange man was playing with his tormentors as a cat plays with a mouse, turning the tables on them in the process.

He picked up the last print and, without glancing at it, placed it face down on the table.

'I am sorry, gentlemen, but this print I refuse to identify.'

He paused and there was another ripple of whispering from the committee and from the newsmen. Cheiro held up his hand for silence.

'Please let me finish! I refuse to identify this print to anyone but the owner . . . because it is the mark of a murderer. He will give himself away through his own self-confidence—and he will largely die in prison from his own anguish.'

Cheiro had been one hundred per cent correct throughout the test. The last print to which he referred in such dramatic fashion had been that of Dr. Henry Meyer, who was then in Tombs prison charged with murder. He was convicted, adjudged insane, and died a few months later in an institution for the criminally insane.

The newspapers were generous with their publicity regarding Cheiro's amazing predictions. People came from all over the world to consult him—at fancy fees. Just what his percentage of error might have been in these cases cannot be told, for they were largely private and no account of them was ever made public.

But there were times when his prophecies were again in the public eye, as in the instance when the eccentric Oscar Wilde, then at the height of his fame, defied Cheiro to work his magic. Cheiro told the famous writer that within five years he would be publicly dishonoured and would send himself into exile. Wilde laughed in his face. Time was on the side of the mystic, however, for within three years the notoriety of Wilde's trial had ruined his career, and he slid swiftly into the dishonour that Cheiro had predicted for him.

Making these deductions from palm-prints was only part of Cheiro's programme, for he also used what he called his mystic numbers. This system was based on the birth date of the subject and the figure selected by the mystic which he called the subject's fatal number.

By whatever process he arrived at this method, he seemed to get results. He predicted the month and year of the death of King Edward VII, and he made his uncanny forecast eleven years before the event. The King kept the prediction locked in his desk. In June of 1902 the King had already been acclaimed by proclamation, but had not yet been crowned. He suddenly became ill, and his condition was so critical that he sent for Cheiro to ask what lay ahead. The palmist told him not to worry, that he would be crowned on August 9th and would live for nine more years. Once again his predictions were fulfilled by the events which followed.

The fame of this remarkable man spread throughout Europe, and he found himself much in demand, especially among Royalty. It was during one of these jaunts that he was in Moscow, where he was asked to read a set of prints on which he predicted: 'The man who made these prints will be unhappy and haunted by fears of war all through his life. About 1917 he will lose everything, including his life.'

He made that prediction in 1897, just twenty years before the owner of the prints, Czar Nicholas, lost both his crown and his life at the hands of the revolutionists in 1917.

Cheiro's astounding ability enabled him to forecast the future for thousands of others, but it mercifully shielded him from a preview of his own. In the autumn of 1906 he found himself having difficulty with his operations. He was no longer sure of himself and his percentage of failures began to rise. Perhaps he needed a rest, he reasoned, so he closed his lavish offices, cancelled his numerous appointments and slipped away to Bermuda for a few weeks.

It was in vain. The gift had deserted him and he could no longer deny it, even to himself. In 1907 he announced that he was retiring. Why not? He had worked hard for many years and had accumulated a sizable fortune in the process of peering into the future. A magazine, a newspaper and a private banking house which he established seemed adequate to keep him busy and prosperous.

Things went well for a time. The wealthy clients who had paid him to guide their business ventures now flocked to his financial institution. But in the winter of 1909 two investors charged that he had vanished with half a million dollars' worth of stock which he had bought for them. He reappeared to defend himself and settled the case out of court. A few months later he faced another charge of the same type. The court found him guilty and sentenced him to prison for thirteen months.

This counsellor of kings and commoners had lost his touch, and the world quickly forgot him. One morning in 1936 the police in Hollywood found him lying on the sidewalk babbling to himself. When they reached the hospital with him he was dead.

The record of this man who called himself Cheiro is no secret, but the talent or the trickery by which he achieved that record is very much a secret. He always maintained that he did not know how he was able to do the amazing things that he did, and it is quite possible that he was telling the truth, for in the final analysis Cheiro the Great was just another baffled, helpless has-been—a magician who had lost his magic.

Pelorus Jack, the Payless Pilot

IF you were an excellent navigator would you guide ships through dangerous waters for forty years without pay?

If you were one of the world's best swimmers would you go back to a job where your only reward was a pistol-shot in the back?

Pelorus Jack was both a navigator and a swimmer. He worked faithfully at his job of guiding ships through dangerous waters for forty years, through fair weather and foul, without losing a ship. No one ever offered to pay him, and Jack never expected to get paid.

Unusual fellow, of course. Most unusual! Pelorus Jack was a porpoise.

Off the coast of New Zealand there is a swift water passage through the D'Urville islands known as French Pass, which extends from Pelorus Sound to Tasman Bay. It is a short cut, albeit a dangerous one. Treacherous currents and jagged underwater rocks lie in wait for the hapless and unwary. It had a bad reputation among seafaring men—until Pelorus Jack came along. Then for forty years it was safe enough, thanks to this remarkable porpoise.

The schooner *Brindle*, out of Boston for Sydney with a load of machinery and shoes, was picking her way gingerly through the Pass one stormy morning in 1871. The crew noticed an unusually large blue-grey porpoise playing along in front of the bow, leaping out of the water and acting like a puppy that is overjoyed at finding a friend. Some of the crew members mistook the porpoise for a young whale calf and they wanted to harpoon it, but the captain's wife prevented it, fortunately. By merely groping along through the mist and rain behind the playful porpoise, the *Brindle* had deep water under her keel all the way through the Pass.

As far as the records are concerned, this trip with the *Brindle* marked the beginning of a self-appointed career for this friendly porpoise. Since he hung around Pelorus Sound, he soon became known as Pelorus Jack and his fame spread around the world, thanks to grateful sailors who credited him with granting them safe passage through those risky waters. For forty years Jack met the ships and leaped out of the water in greeting. The sailors and passengers watched for him and gave him a rousing cheer when he appeared, for with him on the job the threat of French Pass was nullified. The big porpoise played along beside the ships, leaping gracefully into the air. He had no difficulty in keeping up with them, for the porpoise is one of the fastest creatures in the water. Jack would race alongside for miles, crossing under the ships to reappear on the other side at intervals, but once the craft drew near the foaming waters of the Pass, Jack spurted ahead of the bow and stayed there in sight of the pilot, marking the channel until the danger was behind.

In 1903 a drunken passenger on the *Penguin* nicked Jack with a pistol bullet. The crew wanted to lynch the drunk and had to be forcibly prevented from carrying out their threats. Jack failed to report for duty for two weeks and was believed dead—then one bright morning he showed up again, the payless pilot of French Pass. The council at Wellington passed an ordinance protecting Jack from molestation of any kind and empowered sailors to see that the law was enforced, a task they gladly assumed.

After the passenger on the *Penguin* shot him, Jack never met that vessel again—the only craft he refused to accompany. Sailors refused to sign on the *Penguin*. It was jinxed, they said. However that may be, the *Penguin* was wrecked in the Pass in 1909, with heavy loss of life.

Jack was faithful, but he was getting old. Since he had first appeared on his self-assigned task in 1871 Jack had become world-famous. Maritime experts estimated that by conducting thousands of ships safely through the treacherous waters of French Pass, this friendly porpoise had been instrumental in saving countless thousands of lives.

Pelorus Jack was on the job day and night from 1871 until April of 1912. Then, as dramatically as he had appeared, Jack vanished. He was probably the victim of age and his natural enemies. Since Jack had never trained a replacement, his passing left a vacancy that was never filled.

Pelorus Jack had no precedent and no successor, but he does have a safety record unequalled in the annals of the sea, suitably engraved on the statue erected in his memory at Wellington by the grateful sailors and shipowners who benefited from his devotion to duty.

The Curse of the 'Scharnhorst'

FORTY thousand tons of fighting fury that turned out to be forty thousand tons of jinx—that was the *Scharnhorst*.

Hitler's scientists put everything they had into this sleek new battle wagon: speed to outrun the heavier British dreadnoughts; long-range rifles to strike lethal blows over the horizon; powerful electronic gear to find and finish her opponents. All these things they built into her—but they were not enough, for the *Scharnhorst* was hoodooed, so her crewmen said.

The first indication that she was a trouble-maker came while the Nazi technicians were building her. The ship was only about half built when she suddenly groaned and rolled over on her side, crushing sixty workmen to death and injuring a hundred and ten more. Raising her took three months. Crews of workmen had to be drafted to complete her, for the word got around that this steel monster was jinxed, as indeed she may have been.

Came the day for the launching. A major celebration was in order, for the Nazis wanted to impress the world with their skill in contriving new and more deadly forms of seagoing weapons. Hitler would be there, of course, and Goering and Himmler and Doenitz. Yes, they would all be there—and they were there—but one thing was missing: the centre of attraction was not there. The *Scharnhorst* had launched herself during the night, grinding up a pair of huge barges as she lurched towards the channel. The

Nazis had an alibi for that one, too. They told the world that the launching had actually been carried out at night because they had a new and secret method of sliding their sea giants into the water! If that yarn concealed no secrets, at least it covered some red faces.

She was finally at sea, hoodoo and all.

The world first got a glimpse of her in action when she lay in the harbour of Danzig, pumping hundreds of tons of death and destruction into that helpless city. The Germans flooded the world with those newsreel pictures, but they failed to mention that while this roaring monster was belching its fury at the people of Danzig, one of the *Scharnhorst's* big guns exploded and in another gun turret the air system suddenly quit working and twelve men smothered to death.

The jinx ship lost her crews frequently by death and desertion. Every German sailor dreaded assignment to that ill-starred contraption.

When the Nazi battleships poured their fire into the forts of Oslo, the *Scharnhorst* took more shells than all the rest of the fleet combined. She was afire in thirty places when the *Gneisenau* left the battle to pull her to safety, beyond the range of the shore batteries.

Limping along towards home, crippled as she was, the *Scharnhorst* made poor time, for it was a matter of hiding from the British bombers by day and creeping along the coast by night. But at last they got her into the Elbe river, the last lap towards home and safety of a sort. Gliding up the river in total darkness, her radar failed to show the gigantic bulk of a great ocean liner that suddenly loomed up in the narrow channel. Too late the watch sounded the alarm—he died seconds later when the battleship rammed into the mighty *Bremen*. The *Scharnhorst* backed away and crept on upstream, but the pride of the German passenger fleet sank and settled into the mud, where the British finally found her and pounded her to junk with aerial bombs. Germans shook their heads and muttered that the *Bremen* had merely got in the way of the jinx that plagued the *Scharnhorst*.

Hitler's star was flickering when the *Scharnhorst* was ready for action again. The gigantic *Bismarck* had gone down under the guns of the British fleet; the *Tirpitz* was riddled with torpedoes: Hitler had no choice but to send out the *Scharnhorst*, jinx and all.

She slipped down the Elbe, past the rusting ruins of the *Bremen* and northward along the coast of Norway, churning the cold, black waters of the long Arctic night to a froth as she hurried to her rendezvous with destiny.

The *Scharnhorst* had been ordered to plunder our convoys around the northern tip of Norway—convoys that would be fat with vital war materials for Russia, waddling along with little protection. It looked like a cinch; the *Scharnhorst* would not be expected and the flimsy destroyers would be no match for her. A sudden lunge out of the blackness, ripping the convoy to pieces, then back down the coast to a secret base in one of the sheltered fiords before the befuddled British could get their battle fleet into action. The skipper of the *Scharnhorst* was jubilant over the prospects.

The jinx was lying in wait.

A British patrol boat was lying dead in the water, engines disabled. The same blackness that hid the battle wagon also hid her Nemesis, for the *Scharnhorst* pounded past within a few hundred yards of the patrol boat and never saw her. As soon as the battleship was safely over the horizon, the patrol boat flashed the alarm —a German dreadnought on the loose, headed north at full speed. Within a matter of minutes a British fleet had wheeled about and was driving full speed towards the most likely point of contact. If the Germans were sending out a lone battleship, it meant that they were desperate, and it also meant that the attack would be made on our convoys as near as possible to bases where the battleship could hide.

The British made contact with the *Scharnhorst* in the darkness, fought a few minutes and then lost her again, for the German ship was too fast for her potbellied adversaries. The *Scharnhorst* pounded onward towards the area where the convoy was known to be lumbering along. A few hours more and her mission would be accomplished. Only a few hours—but time ran out swiftly. The

British commander had spread his ships in a great fan, probing the darkness for the enemy. A destroyer got a fleeting glimpse ... then lost her again in the mountainous waves. Another glimpse was flashed from a cruiser. Range sixteen thousand yards. The gun crews were ready. The British commander knew that the Germans were taking evasive action. They would turn—but which way?

He guessed and fired.

Miles away in the icy blackness the *Scharnhorst* swung directly into the path of the tons of high explosive that ripped her apart. She staggered under the impact as the shells tore into her vitals. Fires broke out; she lurched along at half speed, and even that could not be maintained, for thousands of tons of water were pouring in. It was only a matter of minutes before she rolled over and plunged to the bottom about sixty miles off the coast of Norway.

In the darkness a few of her crew managed to get away on rafts, to be picked up later by the British, but most of them died in the bitterly cold water before help could reach them.

At least two of the crew managed to reach a tiny rocky island where they made a windbreak out of their raft. Years later they were found, dead from the explosion of their little emergency oil stove.

They had eluded the cold and the British, but they couldn't escape the jinx of the *Scharnhorst*.

The Amazing Prophecy of St. Odelia

IN the closing months of World War II long lines of American tanks rumbled through the little town of Odelianburg in the mountains a few miles west of Strasbourg. These ponderous war machines thundered along within a few yards of a quaint old church and churchyard in which is located the grave of St. Odelia, a gentle, devout woman who predicted the coming of these tanks more than a thousand years before, if you believe in prophecies.

Did she have, for a brief spell, the ability to lift the curtain of time and peer into the future? Did she describe, in the eighth century, the holocaust that swept the world in the twentieth century? Fortune-tellers, spirit mediums, palmists, tea-leaf readers —the list of those who claim to be able to envision the future is long and varied, but St. Odelia belonged to none of these groups.

She was the daughter of wealthy German parents. Born in the year 660, she was blind for almost sixty years. When baptized in the year 719 she reportedly became able to see. Many legends have attached themselves to her, but none stranger than those which spring from an unusual document known as 'St Odelia's Prophecy', which was not intended as a prophecy at all, but was in reality two letters written to her beloved brother, the Prince of Franconia, to describe a series of persistent and recurring dreams she had been experiencing.

Those who saw in these letters a description of World War I found many inconsistencies; the pattern did not fit the product. But this 'prophecy' draws so many apparent parallels with the men and events of World War II that it merits examination for curiosity, if nothing more.

Here, then, are the two strange letters which St. Odelia sent to her brother, transcribed from the Latin in which they were written more than twelve hundred years ago.

'Listen, O my brother, for I have seen the terror of the forests and the mountains. Fear has seized upon the people, because never in any region of the universe has anyone given testimony of such trouble.

The time will come when Germany will be called the most belligerent nation of the world. The period has arrived when out of her bosom will come a terrible warrior to spread war in the world. Men will call him the Antichrist. He will be cursed by mothers by thousands, who will lament like Rachel over the fate of their children, and who will refuse consolation because they will no longer be of this world and will be devastated in their homes.'

Let us turn from her writings for a moment to analyse and compare this first portion of the 'prophecy' with the events.

To say that Germany has become known as the most warlike nation on earth would require no stretch of the imagination, for she was called that, and worse, by the leaders of many nations who had felt her mailed fist. Twice in twenty-five years the Germans plunged the world into war, the most devastating wars in all recorded history.

St. Odelia tells her brother that men will call the leader of the German forces the Antichrist—and Adolf Hitler was indeed called that, for it was a title he earned by his infamous actions. Churches and Church leaders were special objects of persecution. He burned and pillaged and ravaged without cessation as long as he had the power to issue orders. Godliness, by his orders, was made a laughing-stock in the schools of the Hitler Youth Movement. The Ten Commandments were publicly derided and labelled signs of weakness and decay. Hitler deliberately set about destroying the works and teachings of the Gentle Man of Galilee, in order to set himself up as a god before the German people.

Then, says the letter, this fellow will be cursed by thousands of mothers, lamenting the fate of their children.

How terribly true that was! But not thousands of mothers—millions! The mothers of the little children who were herded into the churches of Russia and Poland and burned alive. The mothers of the little girls who were dragged from their homes and hauled away to brothels in German-held territories. And this German leader was cursed, too, by the brokenhearted mothers of Britain and France and Russia and the United States and Australia who saw their sons and daughters march away to give their lives in the struggle with this monster.

But—did St. Odelia really refer to Hitler?

The next paragraph of her first letter gives us a clue. She writes:

'The Conqueror will come from the banks of the Danube. He will be a remarkable chief among men. The war that he brings will be the most terrifying that men have ever undertaken.'

Let's break that down into its various components.

'He will come from the banks of the Danube.' Adolf Hitler was born within fifty feet of the Danube River.

'He will be a remarkable chief among men.' Hitler, the bastard son of uncouth ancestry, slugging, conniving, worming his way ever upward to eventual command of one of the mightiest fighting forces the world had ever seen. Trampling nations underfoot, dominating millions of enslaved peoples, matching wits with Europe's craftiest statesmen and forcing them to bow to his will. Do these things fulfil the requirements for 'a remarkable chief'?

Then says the letter: This war which he brings—'will be the most terrifying that men have ever undertaken'.

World War II was the costliest war ever fought in terms of lives and money. It was indeed the most terrifying conflict in history.

'His arms,' says St. Odelia, 'will be flamboyant, and the helmets of his soldiers will bear points darting flashes of light, while their hands carry lighted torches. It will be impossible to estimate the number of cruelties committed.'

Blazing guns, flame-throwers, firebombs—it all adds up to flamboyant in the sense of the word as St. Odelia used it. The lighted torches we might consider as symbolic of the fires which ravaged city after city, nation after nation, as the legions of Hitler rolled along on their earlier conquests. He strode through the world with a torch in his hand and left it in flames behind him to mark his passing.

'It will be impossible to estimate the number of cruelties committed.' Lidice . . . Dachau . . . The butchery of an entire city . . . The gas oven where millions of helpless human beings were rendered into chemical by-products for Hitler's war machine.

'He will be victorious on land and sea and in the air—because one will see winged warriors in these unbelievable attacks, mounting to the heavens to seize the very stars and throw them down on the cities from one end of the universe to the other in order to start great fires.'

For two whole years after Hitler unleashed his war machine on the world his armed might rolled over the continent of Europe. His swarms of planes annihilated the enemy and drove them from the skies. They made the night brilliant with their flares as they loosed their incendiaries on their defenceless targets.

St. Odelia then warned her brother that the nations of the earth would be astonished at this display of apparently invincible power and would exclaim: 'Whence comes this force? How is he able to undertake such a war?'

To say that the other nations were astonished is no overstatement. Around the globe, the self-appointed experts of contiguous lands laughed at reports of German military strength. There were widely published stories of wooden tanks and guns used in Nazi parades in Berlin, of planes that were hastily flown from one airfield to another in order to conceal scarcity under a false mantle of abundance. Foolish military authorities took pencil and paper and turned out reams of statistics which 'proved' that Hitler could not fight six months because he would run out of oil and gasoline. And wiseacre politicians both here and abroad sneered at the suggestion that France might fall, that Britain would be battered to her knees, that enemy submarines would menace shipping in the mouths of American harbours.

While Germany was coiling 'to strike, false prophets were lulling their complacent listeners with twaddle. Their pet expression was that it was 'a phoney war', but the phoniest part of it was the 'information' the counterfeit statesmen dished out so freely and so disastrously.

Yes, the other nations of the world were astonished, just as St. Odelia had written twelve centuries before.

Her letter continues:

'The earth will tremble with the shock of the fighting. The rivers will run red with blood. Sea monsters will disperse to the top of the oceans.'

Millions of tons of high explosives kept the earth trembling for more than five terrible years. Submarines, surging to the tops of the oceans, would have looked like strange sea monsters to anyone in the eighth century.

'Future generations will be astonished that his numerous and powerful enemies will not have been capable of stopping the march of his victories. And the war will be long.'

The impotence of Hitler's adversaries was a matter of profound surprise which may well carry over into future discussions of the matter. For almost three years after Hitler opened hostilities his opponents suffered a string of almost unbroken defeats, for they had been caught napping. 'And the war will be long.' When Hitler's subordinates surrendered what was left of his holdings in April of 1945, Britain was in her sixth year of fighting with him.

This unusual document continues:

'The conqueror will have attained the apogee of his triumphs towards the middle of the sixth month of the second year of hostilities. This will be the end of the first period of bloody victories. He will say, "Accept the yoke of my domination," while continuing his victories. But his enemies will not submit and he will cry out—"Misfortune will befall them because I am the conqueror." '

Let's analyse that and compare it with the record.

World War II began in September of 1939. The second year of fighting, therefore, began in September of 1940. Six months from that date was March of 1941, a fateful date for Hitler. After that time he never overran another major nation, and in June of 1941 he began his ill-fated attack on Russia. It was the beginning of the end for the Nazis. Hitler tried to throw his yoke over the captured nations but they refused to submit. From their hideouts in forests, mountains, caves and cellars they worked for the day when they could rise again. Was St. Odelia right once more?

In September of 1942 Adolf Hitler spoke to the German Reich from Berlin. He said: 'The enemy will be annihilated. It is fated for Germany to dominate, to rule! I promise you this—it is mine to give to you!' St. Odelia said that the words would be 'Misfortune will befall them. . . . I am the conqueror!' And she said it more than a thousand years before.

Then St. Odelia slips up, if she was describing World War II, for she writes:

'The second part of the war will be equal in length to half of the first part. They will call it the period of diminution. It will be full of surprises which will make the earth tremble, when twenty belligerent nations will clash. Towards the middle of this period the little nations will cry out for peace, but there will be no peace for these nations.'

It is true that we fought a war of attrition against Hitler, but the time element in her letters does not coincide with the period of diminution as it actually developed. By her calculations it would have amounted to a period of nine months, but in reality it amounted to several years. This was the time when we were forging our economic blockade around Germany and demolishing their submarine fleet in the inexorable tightening process. St. Odelia mentions surprises, and there were plenty of those: rocket planes, robot bombs, jet planes, radar. Twenty nations will clash? There were more than twenty, and there were little nations who cried for peace and found none.

'The third period of the war will be the shortest of all, and the conqueror will have lost faith in his warriors. This will be called the period of the invasion, because by just retribution the soil of the conqueror, by reason of his injustice and his atheism, will be invaded in all parts and pillaged. Around the mountains torrents of blood will flow. Then will see a revolt of the women of his nation who will wish to stone him.'

The third period of the war, 'the period of the invasion', was short and terrible. From D-Day in June of 1944 Hitler's days were numbered, and the ultimate conclusion was never in doubt. His generals had tried to assassinate him; the women of Germany had rioted several times in protest and defiance of Hitler. In November of 1944 scores of women at Cologne were executed for the 'crime' of holding peace demonstrations. Germany was in the process of being invaded in all parts and pillaged by the very peoples she had trampled underfoot.

And in conclusion, St. Odelia says:

'But one will also see prodigies in the Orient, where the troops of the Conqueror will be stricken with a strange and unknown illness. This evil will discourage his soldiers, while the nations will say: "The finger of God is there. It is a just retribution."'

Prodigies in the Orient?

For the first time in history the fury of the atomic explosion was unleashed on Hiroshima and Nagasaki. It was a strange and unknown illness that afflicted its victims—and left them discouraged. Was this her way of describing an historic event that was still twelve hundred years in the future when she dreamed of it?

After the fall of the Conqueror and the prodigies in the Orient —what next? St. Odelia says: 'This will not be the end of these wars, but the beginning of the end. . . .'

Korea. . . .

Indo-China. . . .

What next?

St. Odelia doesn't say.

The Man From Nowhere

In marked contrast to the disappearance of Oliver Larch is the equally mystifying appearance of Kaspar Hauser.

The good folk of Nuremberg, Germany, were observing the holiday of Whit Monday in 1828. It was just another day of rest —until someone noticed a strange-looking lad stumbling along just inside the New Gate entrance. He was clean, but poorly dressed, almost ragged. And he had such difficulty in walking that it was first thought he was crippled. His feet were swollen. When an inquisitive policeman tried to question him he only repeated, 'I want to be a soldier like my father was!' From the manner in which he spoke the words it was clear that they meant nothing to him; it was merely something he had been taught to recite.

The officer took him to the police station.

While the Mayor and other local dignitaries crowded round him, this unusual young man continued to mouth his desire to be a soldier. His name? He did not seem to understand, but when a paper and quill pen were placed before him he giggled nervously and wrote in a slow legible hand: Kaspar Hauser. He could not —or would not—write anything else. The entire period of questioning him brought forth only the name Kaspar Hauser and his babbling that he wanted to be a soldier like his father.

There was still another aspect of this mysterious young man

with which the authorities had to deal. He finally produced two letters, one of them dated sixteen years before and purportedly written by his mother. It asserted that she was abandoning him and asked the finder to please send him to Nuremberg when he was seventeen, in order that he might enlist in the Sixth Cavalry, of which his father had been a member. The other letter allegedly was from the finder of the infant, claiming that he had ten children of his own and was no longer able to support Kaspar.

Confronted with this enigmatic holiday development, the officials of Nuremberg decided to sleep on it. They bundled the young man off to the home of the city's most learned citizen, Professor Daumer, where Kaspar astounded that worthy gentleman by trying to pick the flame off a candle. It also developed that the boy had no depth perception at all; he was unable to tell which of two objects was closer to him. He seemed to be in full possession of his faculties, but they were as undeveloped as those of a baby.

The authorities promptly launched an investigation to learn more about their strange young charge. Weeks of questioning, however, failed to develop a single lead. Nobody had seen him approaching the entrance to the city, nor had he been seen on the high road leading to the gate. Yet he had obviously walked a considerable distance to judge from the condition of his feet and legs when he was first noticed. The more the authorities probed, the more confusing the matter became. A reward was posted; pictures of Hauser were distributed far and wide. All over Europe the riddle of Kaspar Hauser became a favourite topic of conversation.

Back in Nuremberg, the subject of all this excitement was busy learning to speak. Professor Daumer and his wife found Kaspar a willing student—incredibly so. In a matter of a year he had learned to speak well enough to be able to tell his benefactors that he had been raised, ever since he could remember, in a dark room or cellar. He had seldom heard speech, had been in contact with only one person in all those years, a man whom he never saw in the light and therefore could not recognize. There was one occasion, according to his account, when he had been punished for being noisy. But where he had been kept, and by whom or why, remained a deep, dark secret, as it does to this day.

In Kaspar Hauser's own story of his life, written about a year after he appeared on the streets of Nuremberg, he repeated most of what was already known from his verbal account, with the addition of a few details which were unusual if not important. For instance, he says that not only did he have no idea of time and no sense of perspective, but that he had no conception of sex or distance. Never having walked beyond the confines of his blackened room, he had difficulty in using his feet and legs. At the time he came to Nuremberg he had never tasted any food other than black bread and water, and it made him quite ill to partake of other foods until many months of freedom had elapsed.

His dramatic and unexplained arrival from nowhere was only the beginning of the strange story of Kaspar Hauser. On October 17, 1829, about eighteen months after he came to Nuremberg, he was found staggering around in the basement of Professor Daumer's house, suffering from a long slash across the forehead. Questioned, Kaspar claimed that he had gone to the basement for some firewood, and that a man wearing a black mask had jumped out from behind a door and stabbed him.

After this incident two policemen were assigned to guard him round the clock. For several months there was nothing worthy of note, then in May, 1831, one of the policemen heard a pistol-shot from Kaspar's bedroom. Rushing in, he found his charge again wounded in the forehead. Accidental, said Kaspar. He told the police that he had been standing on a chair, reaching for a book, and had slipped. In falling, he claimed he had clutched at a pistol hanging on the wall and had accidentally discharged it, inflicting a slight wound.

Near the home of Professor Daumer was a public park. It contained a few trees and a small pond. In summer its principal attraction was the numerous benches where idlers whiled away the time. In winter it was rather bleak and uninviting, but winter or summer Kaspar Hauser made it a practice to take a stroll through that park each day.

Thus it was that on December 14, 1833, he had been gone from Daumer's house only a few minutes when he came staggering out of the park crying for help. He had been stabbed. Two physicians were summoned, and while they worked over their dying patient, several police searched the park for some trace of the attacker.

The doctors found that the weapon, whatever it was, had entered Hauser's back below the rib cage, ranging upward through the diaphragm into the lower portion of his heart. Surrounded by a room full of the curious and the officious, Kaspar Hauser died. Two of the physicians pronounced it a clear case of murder, since in their opinion the location and extent of the wound ruled out the possibility that it might have been self-inflicted. The third doctor did not agree with his colleagues; after considerable soul-searching he expressed the belief that it might have been done by a left-handed person.

If it was murder, the killer was never caught. If Hauser did it himself, he also performed the amazing feat of concealing the weapon so quickly and so thoroughly that it was never found.

Strange things also happened to those who had been close to Hauser. Soon after his death Mayor Binder, Dr. Osterhauser, Dr. Albert and Dr. Prcu also died—and so suddenly that rumour had it they were poisoned.

The known facts in the recorded life of Kaspar Hauser are scanty but sufficient to place him in the records as one of the strangest cases of its kind. It was never learned where he came from, how he got to Nuremberg, nor in precisely what manner he died. Kaspar Hauser was a most unconventional creature, especially to those who knew him best. One of those was von Feurbach, who wrote of him:

'Kaspar Hauser showed such an utter deficiency of words and ideas, such perfect ignorance of the commonest things and appearances of Nature, and such horror of all customs, conveniences, and necessities of civilized life, and, withal, such extraordinary peculiarities in his social, mental, and physical disposition, that one might feel oneself driven to the alternative of believing him to be a citizen of another planet, transferred by some miracle to our own.'

John Keely's Mystery Motor

THE little brick building began to quiver. From the heavy steel machine bolted to the great stone base the hum changed to a moan, and the moan became a whine, which in its turn became an ear-torturing screech of metal in travail. The little window-panes were dancing in their frames as if they were eager to flee from this unearthly din.

John Keely never glanced at the nine men who were crowded into the little room beside him. He pretended not to notice the men, just as he ignored the sound that filled the room. He was the master of the situation, because he was the master of the machine before them. They were demanding proof that their money had gone into something practical. Very well, they would soon have their proof.

He played the scene for all it was worth—then he leaned forward and with his huge forefinger lightly tapped a button.

There was a roar that jarred the bones of every man present. When the faint blue fog had cleared away, the committee members could see that a one-inch lead ball had been driven from the tube on the machine with such terrific force that it had passed completely through two heavy oak planks and buried itself in a sandbox against the wall.

'Most impressive, sir,' said one of the witnesses, 'but when do you expect to put all this latent power to work in a machine which will bring in a few profits to your stockholders?'

For John Ernest Worrall Keely this session with the stockholders' committee in November of 1879 was an old, old story. He gave them performance and they insisted on profits. Surely there must have been times when he regretted having turned his strange talents to the field of invention. But if such occasions developed, he never mentioned them. Through the years of ambivalence that surged about him, John Keely never lost his temper. Nor did he ever lose his ability to find new financial backers when the old ones wore out.

There was little in his youthful background to indicate that he was qualified or inclined towards mechanical ingenuity. Born in Philadelphia in 1827, he worked as a carpenter, played violin in a little orchestra, showed amazing dexterity with card tricks and other paraphernalia of the magician's trade. John longed for adventure and joined with a group of trappers who spent three years in the Rockies. Badly wounded by an Indian arrow, John came home to the relative safety of Philadelphia.

He brought with him his magnetic personality and a versatility which friends called remarkable. In spite of his shortcomings in the field of formal education, young Keely made friends with mechanics and professors and within a few years had acquired smatterings of the fundamentals of both science and machinery.

It was an age when the search for controllable power was spurred by the increasing need for it. Water power was inadequate to the needs of a burgeoning industrial nation. Steam power was capable of meeting the needs, but it was by no means ideal. There was a great demand for some cheap source of energy that could be put to work turning the wheels of a nation that was just beginning to realize its potential.

John Keely first attracted nationwide attention in 1873 when he made the dramatic and surprising assertion that he had found and tapped that great new source of energy that America needed. What was it? The inventor was exasperatingly vague. He said: 'I have been working on a device which disintegrates the etheric force which controls the atomic constitution of matter. I have been able to apply this force through my motor by means of induced harmonic vibrations.'

When his contemporaries called for more enlightening details of this revolutionary process, Keely showered them with a barrage of theories and explanations which were at variance with the accepted scientific views. A few scientists challenged him, a few denounced him, but most of them adopted a policy of watchful waiting. If he failed to produce some proof of his claims, there would be time enough for ridicule.

Keely confounded his critics by giving demonstrations which won substantial financial support. He invited a select group of witnesses, carefully placing the newspaper correspondents in the most prominent positions, and they saw his machine tear a two-inch hawser into shreds. How was it accomplished? The inventor launched into an 'explanation' which was something less than understandable. He assured them that they were observing the powers of a hydro-pneumatic-pulsating-vacue engine. Be that as it may, the witnesses went away having seen a large and complicated device which exhibited powers beyond that of any similar creation of its time.

Some of the most prominent business men in Philadelphia and New York invested their money in Keely's unusual device. If, as he seemed to prove, he could concentrate the little-understood forces of Nature into a machine which could convert these forces into controllable energy, then there was almost no limit to the profits that could be made. The Keely Motor Company was born and $100,000 was subscribed. More was available, but Keely drew the line at the hundred-thousand-dollar mark. That would be ample, he said.

Sixty thousand of the stockholders' dollars went at once into the construction of a new and more powerful machine. It had just one shortcoming—it did not work. The irate stockholders refused to sink any more money into it, and Keely simply bade them adieu while new investors poured fresh funds into his operations.

L

For the next seven years he produced one machine after another and the machines, in their turn, produced astonishing results when called upon to do so. They could drive drills through steel as though it were cheese, a feat which no other device of the period could even approach. Scores of privileged spectators saw Keely's mechanical monsters jerk cables apart, twist heavy iron bars into corkscrews, or stretch them into wire. There seemed to be reason to accept his statement that he was on the verge of conquering some tremendous and hitherto undiscovered force. But time after time when the stockholders began to feel that they were also holding the baby, Keely would refuse to permit any exploitation of the machine as it was then developed. He maintained that it was a Frankenstein that might get out of control and wreak incredible damage unless the motivating force was better understood and better controlled. The motivating force of the stockholders was no match for the motivating force of Keely's contentions. The stockholders always suffered defeat.

There is a limit to the patience of even the most faithful stockholders, and in December of 1882 that limit was reached with the investors of the Keely Motor Company. Through their stormy meeting John Keely sat quietly. When they had finished with their fulminations he rose to meet their charges.

Quietly and with a dignity in marked contrast to the manner of those who had preceded him, Keely stated his case:

'It has been charged that I refuse to reveal the secret of my motor, and that charge I accept as true. I do refuse to reveal the secret. I refuse because, in so refusing, I am protecting not only myself but those who have put their faith and their money in my motor. I shall not betray the trust of those who merit my trust. I will not, without your prior knowledge and consent, publicly divulge the manner in which this motor is energized. I will, however, gladly reveal that information to any representative whom you may select.'

The stockholders selected a gentleman named Edward Boekel, who was known to them as an authority on steam engines and was generally acknowledged to be well informed on matters of science.

Boekel was taken into Keely's confidence, so he reported to the stockholders, and was given an insight into the secret of the motor's strange powers. He said: 'Although I was not fully conversant with all of the factors involved in this machine, I saw and understood more than enough to satisfy myself that Mr. Keely had discovered all that he had claimed.' Thus mollified, the stockholders retired to another period of waiting—and worrying.

What Keely discovered, if he discovered anything, is by no means clear. He repeatedly gave demonstrations at which his various machines amazed and at times alarmed the spectators. In August of 1883 he invited a group of professors and stockholders to one of these mechanistic seances. When they were all seated he dimmed the lights and the great engine in the centre of the room began to pulsate with some awesome force. Valves opened and hissed, whistles blew, and smoke and steam squirted out of obscure orifices. Keely, wearing a leather apron and carrying a block of iron in a pair of heavy tongs, advanced on the machine and carefully placed the iron in its innards, so that it was held between two huge clamps.

After a few more minutes of the snorting, whistling and fuming, the block of iron began to glow redly. Keely was all over the place busily adjusting knobs and pulling levers, evidently enjoying himself immensely.

One of his spectators, Dr. Anjus Andresen, wrote of it later:

'It was like a scene from a frightening theatrical performance. One could shut one's eyes and imagine oneself in the nether regions. And upon opening the eyes the impression was heightened by the spectacle of this massive conglomeration of pipes and levers and the brightly glowing bar of iron which the thing seemed to be holding in its mouth, while at the same time Mr. Keely would have sufficed in the role of His Satanic Majesty.'

The purpose of this impressive demonstration was to show the visitors that the machine could take a piece of cold iron and force it into the shape of a railroad rail, which no contemporary device could do, according to Keely. But, once the demonstration had been concluded, he was vague about plans for putting the machine on the market, and nothing came of it, as usual.

The angry stockholders were soon swarming about him again, and in 1885 he managed to stand them off in court. But the day of reckoning was not far away, and Keely probably knew it, for he plunged into his labours with renewed zeal. Between 1885 and 1888 he made more than seventy devices, testing some before witnesses, destroying others after a few runs seen only by himself and his machinists. There were periodic announcements that the Keely Motor Company's wonderful machine was about ready for the market. On such occasions the stock would fluctuate wildly. It zoomed to two hundred a few times and once reached almost a thousand dollars per share. The stockholders who knew when to buy and when to sell never worried about the machine—they did all right for themselves without it.

A group of disgruntled shareholders hired a committee of experts to investigate this machine for them and in 1888, after Keely had persistently refused to permit the examination, they took the case to court. Keely ignored the court's order to permit the examination and as a result he went to jail.

After this experience he decided that he had had more than his share of troubles with stockholders. He no longer needed them, for he had found a champion in the person of Clara Jessup, wealthy widow, author and philanthropist. She guaranteed him a salary of $2,500 per year and she paid for the experiments, a tidy little matter of more than a hundred thousand dollars.

The jail sentence was the turning-point in Mr. Keely's amazing career. He rid himself of the trouble-makers, but something within the man himself also deserted him. From that time forward to the end of his life in 1898, John Keely talked like a man who was trying to sell himself a bill of goods, as he may have been. His experiments were a series of broken machines that were destroyed in fits of temper before they were completed. He babbled to newspapermen of 'polar sympathies', 'molecular disintegration', 'de-polar waves of force' and the like.

If Keely was the discoverer of some new source of power, he was never able (or willing) to disclose the proof to his contemporaries. If he was a fraud, as many claimed, the proof of his fraud was not established beyond reasonable doubt. Although he used more than a million dollars of stockholders' money during his amazing twenty-five-year career, Keely himself lived plainly, almost frugally, and he left an estate of only fifteen hundred dollars.

Even in death he was plagued by the stockholders, who continued to probe as always. They wrecked the machine shop where he had toiled so many years. When they came upon a three-ton steel sphere which contained compressed air, they called in newspapermen and announced that they had uncovered the secret of Mr. Keely's amazing motor—he did it all with compressed air!

It mattered not that the use of compressed air was no secret at all, for Keely had upon numerous occasions shown the sphere to interested parties, demonstrating how he used it to drive some of the small tools with which he machined the motors. It did not matter to the irate stockholders that the pipes which connected the compressed-air tank to the shop were only slender brass tubes utterly inadequate to conduct air at the pressures which would have been demanded by such tests as they had witnessed.

Somewhere in that cumbersome description of *hydro-pneumatic-pulsating-vacue* there may have been a clue to the real nature of Keely's source of power. Certainly some of the things his machines did could not be attributed to any power-source of his time. If he was a trickster, he was a far more clever man than the scientists and mechanical experts who sought to expose him. If he really depended on some little-known source of power for his experiments, it must have been a form of energy which he could not explain because he did not understand it himself—a rung of science which he grasped briefly in an unsure hand before it slipped away, never to be found again.

Of John Ernest Worrall Keely the *National Cyclopedia of American Biography* says:

> 'The theory that he was a deliberate and conscienceless exploiter of human credulity hardly comports with his years of industrious experimenting and the patience he expended on the construction of one complicated device after another, many of which were never shown to anyone. . . . He was evidently neither insane nor merely an ordinary swindler. . . . He was a man of irreproachable character.'

The enigma of Keely's motor remains unsolved. The witnesses at his demonstrations all agreed on one thing—that the machine made weird sounds. The question remains, were they hearing the birth pangs of a great discovery—or merely the persuasive hum of a humbug?

The Search for John Paul Jones

I⊤ sounds incredible, but it is true nevertheless, that the American government once dug a mine in the city of Paris in order to find an American admiral.

Fate plays some strange tricks on those whom she has marked for fame, and among the oddest of her vagaries is the case of John Paul Jones, one of the founders of the American Navy.

He was indeed a friend in need. When the colonies were desperate for men to lead their cockleshells against the British fleet, Jones was ready, willing and able. The task appeared hopeless to the point of being suicidal, but he took it on with a vengeance. Precisely—with a vengeance.

He, too, had a score to settle with the British. John Paul Jones was a Scot. His name wasn't even Jones; John Paul had added that as a matter of precaution.

As John Paul he had been captain of a British merchant ship. In 1773 he had a mutinous crew on his hands, and in the fight for control of the vessel John Paul shot to death a member of the crew. Authorities at the port of Tobago decided he would have to stand trial, which meant almost certain death, since he knew the entire crew would testify against him. One night while a heavy thunderstorm was lashing the island, he picked the lock on his cell door and took his leave of the British government.

John Paul, late of His Majesty's Navy, had become John Paul the fugitive.

Slipping into the embattled colonies, John Paul lived with a well-to-do family named Jones—and added their name to his own. He insisted to the public that he was a long-lost cousin of the Jones family, and they helped him out by supporting his contention.

The story of his heroic services to the tiny American fleet is one of the brightest pages in our history. With little more than courage and skill and the admiration of his crew, he outfoxed and outfought the British ships of the line which were sent to hunt him down.

The end of the revolution found him without a job—at least the kind of job that he found to his liking, for John Paul Jones had developed a taste for fighting that matched his aptitude for it. He began to smell powder smoke in the East, and with the rank of rear admiral he joined the Russian Navy. Catherine the Great was proud of his exploits and rightly so, for under his command her ships trounced the highly touted Turks—one of the few major naval victories in the history of Russia.

The life of a mercenary fighter was made to order for him. He drank the wine of victory and revelled in his successes, but the sands were running out for this homeless warrior. In Paris, at the age of forty-five, he died quietly and alone.

One hundred and thirteen years later the American government discovered that one of its heroes was missing. A frantic search disclosed that John Paul Jones had died in Paris. The government had ordered his body embalmed for shipment to the United States, and then had failed to call for the body. It was all pretty humiliating.

Then began one of the strangest government projects ever instituted. First the U.S.A. had to secure permission from the French government to look for their missing hero. They found that the old cemetery in Paris where Jones had been interred had long since been abandoned and covered with hospitals and shops and factories. In the musty archives of Paris someone located a map of the cemetery which showed the approximate location of Jones's body. Knowing that it was there was the least of the difficulties; the real problem was to find it under such conditions.

Miners were employed and they sank a shaft beside a large building a couple of hundred feet from the estimated location of the leaden casket containing Jones's body. The tunnelling continued day after day, around buildings, under them, past several leaden caskets which proved not to be the one they sought.

Late one afternoon a workman felt a dull thud as his pick struck into the clay. Careful excavating brought out the casket—lead—with the initials J.P.J. on the cover. In the presence of experts the lid was carefully cut away. The embalmers had done a magnificent job; the feet and hands were carefully wrapped in metal foil, and the body was so well preserved than an autopsy proved that he had died of Bright's disease, as his death certificate showed. Except for a slight flattening of the nose where the casket had pressed upon it, the likeness between the body and the paintings of Admiral Jones was striking. The strange search was at an end.

Fittingly enough, John Paul Jones came back to rest among other heroes at Annapolis with all the honours that the United States could bestow, escorted by part of the American battle fleet which he had helped to bring into being more than a hundred years before.

The Mare Solved the Mystery

THREE-YEAR-OLD Ronnie Weitcamp left his three small playmates in the front yard and ran around the house. It was a few minutes before noon on October 11th, 1955. Two hours later Ronnie was the object of one of the most intensive searches central Indiana ever saw, a search that led into many states and, finally, to a horse that had the answer.

When little Ronnie failed to come in for lunch on that fateful day, his mother inquired of his three small playmates, who told her, 'Ronnie went into the woods and he wouldn't come out!' Frantic, the mother spread the alarm, for the 'woods' to which the children referred constituted thousands of acres of scrub timber that spread over the hilly south-central Indiana landscape around the Crane Naval Depot where Ronnie's father worked. If Ronnie was lost in there, finding him quickly was imperative.

Sheriff's deputies and Indiana State Police lined up shoulder to shoulder with an estimated fifteen hundred employees of the Naval Depot. Ronnie had been missing only a couple of hours when the first search parties were formed; by late afternoon, when the October chill began to settle over the scene, long lines of men were scanning the bushes and ravines for some trace of the youngster. They were working against time, for without shelter it was highly improbable that Ronnie could live through the night.

When the searchers came in empty handed, long after dark,

the case took a different twist. Ronnie was a very pretty little fellow and very friendly. Had he taken up with some stranger and been abducted? The searchers felt certain that they had not over-looked him. They had tramped through thickets and creeks and gullies for hours, covering far more ground than a three-year-old boy could conceivably encompass in the same period of time. Had he been kidnapped, after all?

Once the story hit the front pages of the newspapers and the broadcast services, tips poured in from all sides. Ronnie was seen in a bus station; he was seen with a young man dressed in a hunting costume walking along a street in an Illinois town about a hundred miles from Crane, Indiana. Authorities were overlook-ing no bets. With the aid of the F.B.I. they ran down every 'clue' and each fruitless tip. Among others, the newspapers played up the yarn of a drunken veterinarian in New Jersey who blabbed that the missing child was buried in the backyard of the Weitcamp home!

As news director of television station WTTV at Bloomington, I was one of the first to be contacted by the authorities in this case, since our Bloomington studios were only about twenty-five miles from the scene of the search. We flashed the picture of Ronnie Weitcamp at two-hour intervals, in the hope that some-one might recognize him and give authorities the lead that would return the child to his grief-stricken parents and his brothers and sisters. I televised an interview with the parents in the faint hope that if the child had been abducted the guilty party might realize the enormity of the crime and return the child. All our efforts were in vain; Ronnie Weitcamp had vanished without a trace.

Eleven days dragged by and still no trace of little Ronnie. Even the 'tips' and 'leads' from persons who thought they had seen him petered out. The story dropped to the inside pages of the Indiana newspapers, to be replaced in the headlines with newer and fresher matters.

On the night of October 22nd, after the search for Ronnie Weitcamp had ground to a halt for lack of any further leads, my wife and I were discussing the matter and she recalled the strange case of a few years before in which authorities in a New England city had credited a most unusual source with helping them solve the mystery of a missing child.

The authorities in that case said they had found the child with information supplied by a talking horse!

When my wife reminded me of the incident, I could recall that I had seen it on the news wires, but I was understandably vague on details. Yet it took only a few minutes' searching through the files of my broadcast scripts to come up with the details:

In Richmond, Virginia, there was a most unusual horse known as Lady Wonder. In response to questions, the horse would use her nose to flip up large tin letters which hung from a bar across her stall. By flipping up these letters she spelled out words in answer to the questions put to her.

When the police authorities of Norfolk County, Massachusetts, had to admit failure in their months-long search for four-year-old Danny Matson, they turned in desperation to Lady Wonder. According to the District Attorney of Quincy, the horse directed them to a water-filled stone quarry which had already been searched without result. But this time, with misgivings, they searched the quarry again and found the body of Danny Matson, exactly as the horse had indicated.

The so-called 'talking horse' had apparently been able to direct the authorities to the missing Danny Matson. Could the same animal do as much in the case of Ronnie Weitcamp?

Since I could not get away to make the trip to Richmond, Virginia, myself, I immediately got in touch by long-distance telephone with a close personal friend in Washington, D.C., about a hundred and seventy-five miles from Richmond. It took considerable persuasion on my part to induce my friend and a companion to make the trip; after all, who wants to drive a hundred and seventy-five miles to talk to a horse?

They went reluctantly. They returned bewildered.

Mrs. Fonda, the owner of the horse, was ill, and Lady Wonder was more than thirty years old, a veritable Methuselah of her species. After convincing Mrs. Fonda that their case was an emergency, my friends were finally permitted to enter the stable to question the horse.

The first question they put to her was, 'Do you know why we are here?'

Without hesitation the horse spelled out 'B-O-Y.'

'Do you know the boy's name?'

Lady Wonder flipped up the letters 'R-O-N-E.' (Was she trying to spell 'Ronnie'?)

'Is he dead or alive?'

'D-E-A-D.'

'Was he kidnapped?'

'N-O.'

'Will he be found?'

'Y-E-S.'

'Where?'

'H-O-L-E-.'

'Is he more than a quarter of a mile from where he was last seen?'

'Y-E-S.'

'More than a mile?'

'N-O.'

'What is near him?'

'E-L-M.'

'What kind of soil?'

'S-A-N-D.'

'When will he be found?'

'D-E-C.'

With that the ancient mare turned and shuffled unsteadily out of the stable, the interview at an end. My friends hastened to the nearest telephone to recount their unusual experience to me.

It was a strange performance, indeed, but to Lady Wonder it was an old, old story.

Mrs. Fonda purchased her in 1925, when she was a two-week-old colt. Shortly thereafter Mrs. Fonda and her husband noticed a most peculiar trait that the colt had developed—she did not wait to be called but came trotting out of the field when either of the Fondas *thought* of calling her. By the time she was two years old Lady Wonder had learned to count and to spell out short words by tumbling children's blocks around with her nose. One day she spelled out the word 'engine' and a moment later a huge tractor came chugging past the house.

The fame of the fabulous mare spread rapidly. Thousands of people came from all parts of the continent to seek answers to their questions. Mrs. Fonda placed a charge of fifty cents per question on their inquiries. Patiently, Lady Wonder nuzzled the tin letters into position to spell out words and sentences. According to the *Chicago Tribune*, the mare predicted that Franklin D. Roosevelt would be the next President of the United States, making the prediction even before F.D.R. had been nominated. She correctly predicted the winners of races (until Mrs. Fonda refused to accept any more questions of that type) and in fourteen out of seventeen years she correctly predicted the winner of the World Series. Lady Wonder sometimes ventured into the field of mathematics, as for instance the time when she quickly gave the cube root of 64 to a group of visiting students. Dr. J. B. Rhine, the famed Duke University specialist in extrasensory perception, spent about two weeks studying and testing Lady Wonder. He and his assistants came away convinced, so they reported, that she had some sort of genuine telepathic powers.

Admittedly, Lady Wonder was a most unusual horse. She had unhesitatingly spelled out answers in reply to the questions my friends had put to her. Did I dare use such material on my television news programme? What would happen if I did use it?

It was a difficult decision for me to make, but I finally decided to broadcast the replies just as Lady Wonder had given them ... for what they might be worth, if anything. All other avenues which might have led to the missing Ronnie Weitcamp had dwindled to nothing. Anything that might lead to his recovery was worth trying at that stage of the search.

On the night of October 24, 1955, I broadcast the strange story of Lady Wonder and her replies to question about Ronnie Weitcamp.

I was the target for editorial ridicule from various newspapers in central Indiana. There was some very pointed criticism, tinged with sneers, from one of the Naval Depot officials who insisted that the missing child was still alive and had been kidnapped.

The weeks dragged along without a trace of little Ronnie.

Then, on the afternoon of Sunday, December 4, two teen-age boys found Ronnie's body. Authorities determined that Ronnie had been dead when Lady Wonder said he was dead; that he had not been kidnapped; that he had died of exposure shortly after he disappeared. The child's body was found in a thicket in a brushy gully or ravine, in sandy soil, a little more than a mile from where he was last seen. There were a few saplings in the vicinity; the nearest tree was an elm about thirty feet from the body. And the child was found in December, just as Lady Wonder had predicted many weeks before.

To those who were familiar with this unusual mare and her past performances, the case of Ronnie Weitcamp was an old, old story. To me, it was by all odds the strangest story that I had ever reported in my thirty-one years of news broadcasting.

The Modern Jonah

Is IT possible for a man to be swallowed by a whale—and live to tell the story?

It is not only possible—it actually happened. All that was necessary was for the right man and the right whale to get together at the right time. According to the records of the British Admiralty, that was what happened when James Bartley, an apprentice seaman on a whaler, met with a huge cachalot whale in February of 1891.

James Bartley was swallowed by a whale and he lived to tell the story.

He was making his first (and last) trip on the whaling ship *Star of the East*. She was pounding along before a fair breeze a few hundred miles east of the Falkland Islands in the South Atlantic.

Suddenly the lookout gave his electrifying cry—the traditional 'She blows—there she blo-o-o-ows!' He had spotted a huge sperm whale half a mile off the port bow. The *Star of the East* slacked her sails and lowered her small boats. The deadly race had begun.

Young James Bartley was in the first longboat to reach the side of the giant mammal. They crept up from the rear, so near that the harpooner could lean over and ram his weapon deep into the whale's vitals before it realized what was happening. Bartley and the other oarsmen backed frantically to get out of the reach of those massive flukes, the two-pronged tail which threshed the water to foam as the stricken beast sought to free itself of the harpoon. Luck was with the boatmen for a moment as the whale sounded. Eight hundred feet of heavy line streaked out of the line tub before the whale stopped his dive. There was an ominous slacking in the line—the monster was coming up—but where? The oarsmen hunched over their oars, ready to literally pull for their lives. Without warning there was a splintering crash which sent their little cockleshell spinning into the air. The whale threshed about blindly, snapping at the men and the wreckage, beating the water to a bloody froth before he sounded again.

Another longboat picked up the survivors, but two men were missing—one of them the apprentice, young James Bartley.

The wind which had brought the *Star of the East* to this point had now deserted her, and for hours she lay becalmed, sails limp, wallowing with the light swell that was running.

Shortly before sunset of that same fateful day, the stricken whale floated to the surface only a few hundred yards from the vessel. The crew hastily fastened a line to the whale, and the winch brought it to the ship, where hot weather made it imperative that it be cut up at once. Having no means of raising it to the deck, the men took their flensing spades and peeled off the blubber as they slipped and slid along the creature's back. It was dangerous work, too, for sharks were swarming about, maddened by the taste of blood in the water.

Late at night, working by lantern-light, the tired crewmen removed the stomach of the whale and slowly winched it to the deck for flensing. They were startled to notice movement inside the giant paunch, movement that looked like something living and breathing. The captain hurriedly called the ship's doctor, and a great incision was carefully made in the tough flesh. Out slid the missing sailor, James Bartley—alive! He was doubled up as though suffering from a severe attack of cramps, and he was unconscious.

For want of anything better, the doctor ordered Bartley drenched with buckets of sea water, a treatment which soon

M

restored consciousness but not reason, for he was babbling incoherently and nonsensically. For several weeks Bartley was confined to a cabin, bound so that he could not injure himself in his wild flounderings. Gradually, so the ship's doctor wrote in his record, Bartley recovered his senses. By the time a month had passed after his frightful experience, the young sailor was able to tell what had happened.

Bartley said that he saw the tremendous mouth open over him and he screamed as he was engulfed by it. There were some sharp stabbing pains as he was swept across the teeth. Then he found himself sliding feet first down a slimy tube that carried him to the mammal's stomach. He could breathe, but the hot, fetid odour soon rendered him unconscious. The last thing he could remember was kicking as hard as he could at the soft, yielding stomach . . . . Then blissful unconsciousness until he came to his senses again almost a month later.

As a result of his fifteen hours inside the stomach of the whale, Bartley lost all the hair on his body and he was blinded for the rest of his life. His skin bleached out into an unnatural whiteness that gave him the appearance of being bloodless, although he was actually quite healthy.

He never made another trip to sea but settled down to a quiet life as a shoe cobbler in his native city of Gloucester, England. Numerous medical experts came to examine him and to discuss with him his incredible experience, but Bartley soon became reluctant even to mention it and finally refused to discuss it at all. He died eighteen years after his remarkable adventure and is buried in the family churchyard at Gloucester. On his tombstone is a brief account of his experience and a footnote which says:

James Bartley   1870-1909   A Modern Jonah

Meriwether Lewis—Murder or Suicide?

BETWEEN the shot that killed Meriwether Lewis and the lucky break that had launched him on his career there are many strange episodes, of which his death itself was but the culmination.

Honoured for his part in the great Lewis and Clark Expedition, and condemned by his political enemies for alleged graft and fraud, Meriwether Lewis came to his death in the ramshackle log cabin of John Griner in the hills of Tennessee under circumstances which are subject to several interpretations. Did he kill himself? Was he murdered? In either case, why?

Let's look at the record.

The tall, gaunt stranger who had asked for lodging at the humble cabin of Mr. and Mrs. John Griner on that October evening in 1809 did not bother to identify himself. He took the room which was offered and ate his evening meal in silence. The Griners were accustomed to providing lodging for occasional travellers and they had learned to ask no questions, for Tennessee was still a wild country that harboured some rough characters.

After supper the stranger retired at once to his room. The Griners heard him muttering, but they could not tell whether he was talking to himself or holding a real or fancied conversation with someone else. Since their own room was in the shed kitchen at the rear of the cabin, it was possible, though not probable, that someone else could have entered the stranger's room. Not probable, however, without the family dogs raising quite a rumpus—and they gave no sign of alarm.

Shortly before dawn the next morning the Griners heard a shot. It seemed to be in the house or very near the house. Mrs. Griner hurriedly unlatched the front door and looked around. She noticed that the dogs were gone, but otherwise everything was as it should have been. From the stranger's room there came groans. She called her husband and together they entered.

They gazed down on a mystery that has never been solved.

The tall stranger was writhing in agony on the floor. His garments were soaked with blood from a wound on the left side. There was a low stump which still stood in the corner of the hurriedly built cabin room and the dying man clutched at it.

Mr. Griner tried to staunch the flow of blood while his wife bathed the stranger's face with a damp cloth. There was little time remaining. The stranger raised himself on one elbow and said, 'I am no coward . . . but it is hard to die . . . so young . . . so hard to die . . .' and sank back down. A few minutes later he was gone.

Who was he? Where did he come from?

The Griners searched through his battered old leather knapsack and found only two well-worn buckskin shirts, a crudely painted picture of a young dark-haired woman and a little ledger which bore on its flyleaf the inscription: 'Meriwether Lewis, Albemarle, Virginia. Capt., U.S. Army.'

Captain Meriwether Lewis of the famed Lewis and Clark Expedition, Governor of the Louisiana Territory, dead on the floor of a cabin, by a gunshot wound of unknown origin!

The Griners had both heard the shot. They had both rushed into the adjoining room in a matter of seconds. They had both noticed that in the small room where Captain Lewis lay dying *there was no powder-smoke*. This was odd, they thought, for the black powder used in those days left an acrid white fog to mark its firing—but there was no such smoke in Lewis's room.

They decided that this was a matter which had best be left to the authorities, such as they were, and Mr. Griner saddled up his mule and rode off to the nearest settlement, some thirty miles away.

At the time of his death, Meriwether Lewis was en route to Washington to defend himself against charges that he had been lax in handling financial affairs in his capacity as Governor of the Louisiana Territory. He had left St. Louis accompanied by Major John Neely of the U.S. Army. As they made their way along the lonely roads in the foothills of eastern Tennessee, several of the pack mules carrying Lewis's records panicked in a thunderstorm and Major Neely went back to catch them. The Governor, thin from malaria and sick at heart from the political calumny that was being heaped upon him, continued until he reached the cabin of the Griners.

The charges against him were later found to be baseless, and perhaps a more patient man might have ridden out the storm with less suffering to the soul, but Meriwether Lewis had long been consumed with another inward fire, that of being frustrated in love. He had been courting the daughter of Vice-President Aaron Burr at the time President Jefferson had sent him off with his friend Lieutenant William Clark on the journey that was to make them famous. Aaron Burr did not approve of his daughter's fondness for Captain Lewis and Lewis suspected that Burr had a hand in sending him away into the wilderness. When Lewis next saw Miss Burr it was at her father's trial for treason at which Lewis's friends were aligned against Burr. The greeting from her for which Lewis had long been waiting was cold. Stunned and saddened by this turn of events, Lewis turned away and left for St. Louis to take up his new duties as Governor of the Territory—a bachelor, but not by choice.

As he started back to Washington to defend himself against his political enemies three years later, Lewis was physically worn and mentally fatigued. Had he lived to reach Washington he could easily have cleared himself of the charges which had been made and in so doing he could, on the basis of the evidence in his ledgers, have scored heavily against his detractors.

Thomas Jefferson accepted the report that this gallant explorer had died by his own hand, presumably in a fit of mental depression.

But the suicide theory left some unanswered questions.

Governor Lewis's rifle was standing in the corner of the room where he died and it had not been fired. There was no powder-smoke in the room when the Griners rushed in a few seconds after hearing the shot. If Lewis killed himself by pistol what became of the weapon? No pistol was ever found although the room was repeatedly searched.

What of Major Neely, the Governor's companion? He went back to catch the mules, so he said, and for some reason he never showed up at the Griner cabin until mid-morning of the following day, hours after Lewis's death. At the time he decided to spend the night with the mules, or wherever he spent it, Major Neely presumably had no way of knowing whether the Governor had found shelter from the storm.

What really happened to this national hero? Did he die by his own hand in a fit of despair? If he shot himself, what did he do with the weapon? Or was Meriwether Lewis murdered by political enemies to enable tnem to rifle his ledgers in order to protect themselves?

His friends failed to provide the answers to those questions and his enemies had good reasons for not wanting them answered, so the tragic end of Meriwether Lewis remains as one of the unexplained mysteries of history, fenced in by question marks.

Disaster at Johnstown

THE history of America is the story of a nation in a hurry. Everything they do must be done a little faster than it was done before; the sailing vessel gave way to the paddle-wheel steamer; the steamers vanished as the noisy little locomotives passed them by. Boilers exploded, trains crashed and burned, but the great American rush never paused. Cities and towns were hastily constructed and promptly deserted. The incessant urge to 'get going' has made its mark on their national character.

It was this same trait which paved the way for one of their greatest disasters, a terrible lesson in the price we pay when we substitute haste for quality.

In the south-western part of Pennsylvania, among the foothills of the blue Alleghenies, there lies a sleepy and picturesque valley. Through it winds the little Conemaugh River. The stream is seldom more than fifty feet wide; swift but not deep. Kids fished in it for perch and catfish in the 1880s, just as they do today. The Conemaugh was a friendly little stream—if you let it alone.

Strung out down the valley were five industrial towns: South Fork, Mineral Point, Conemaugh, Woodvale . . . and the fifth bore a name to remember—Johnstown. Forty thousand people lived in those five little towns, and thirty-five thousand of them lived in Johnstown.

Decoration Day, 1889. Johnstown was the centre of interest.

Bands played in the parks. There was a two-mile-long parade of Civil War veterans, fraternal organizations, and proud city leaders behind their fine horses. It was a grand sight as the procession wound to the cemetery to pay its respects to the honoured dead. Then more speechmaking. And all the while the heavy clouds continued to pile up.

By nightfall the sprinkle had become a downpour. The bunting sagged and streaked around the bandstands. By eleven o'clock the rain was a cloudburst, hour after hour of blinding torrents.

Morning revealed the true state of affairs. Both the Conemaugh and Stony Creek were out of their banks at Johnstown. Water was five feet deep in a couple of the streets.

Both streams had been that high before but this time they continued to rise. Furniture was moved upstairs, families hurriedly doubled up with friends. At noon the water was surging through the business district, three feet deep. By two o'clock the town was wallowing in from five to ten feet of surging yellow flood.

Ten miles up the valley, four hundred and fifty feet above Johnstown, lay Conemaugh Lake. It was an artificial reservoir backed up behind an earthen dam. Four hundred acres of water, fifty feet deep.

The dam was inadequate in the first place, and it was old. The Pennsylvania Railroad had bought the canal which the reservoir supplied, and subsequently sold it to a party of wealthy sportsmen. Being in a hurry to get the repair job done cheaply, they patched the original dam with loose dirt and bales of straw and built a flimsy board covering for the overflow. The spillway was obstructed, the centre of the dam sagged, and the bottom safety valve was plugged. It had been that way for nine years. Now it was ready to pay off in disaster.

Ten miles down the valley lay Johnstown. By noon of the thirty-first the lake was pouring over the top of the miserable dam. Hundreds of persons had gathered there—out of idle curiosity for the most part. They saw water spurting thirty feet into the air through leaks beneath the weakened structure. The water was devouring the dam from above and below. The horrified spectators saw the overflow boards swept away. They saw the water rip off the top of the straw bales and rickety post fillers, and then, in a flash, the dam simply dissolved.

Twenty million tons of water plunging down a four-hundred-and-fifty-foot incline upon the hapless thousands of Johnstown.

The surging torrent leaped to its destiny with a roar that shook the earth. Tearing through the narrow valley at a mile a minute, it swept everything before it. An iron bridge sprang high in the air and vanished in the flood. Morgan's mill simply exploded into kindling wood. Four miles away at South Fork a freight train was standing at the station. Above the hissing of his own engine the engineer heard the roar of doom up the valley. He cut loose from the rest of the train and yanked the throttle open. Whistle wailing, the little engine strained to outdistance the fingers of the flood; a mile, a mile and a half, and suddenly the wall of water engulfed it.

At Mineral Point another engineer sensed his danger and broke loose in a wild flight. He had a two-minute start and a downgrade. With the whistle screaming a warning, the crew of Number 59 fired that engine as it had never been fired before. They were hemmed in by the raging river on one side and high cliff walls on the other. Death was only a few hundred yards behind.

Number 59 streaked into the Johnstown yards with less than a minute to spare. The whistle was tied down, a warning to the stricken city, but a warning that few had time to heed. The engineer fell into a deep ditch with hundreds of others and the fireman was tossed high in the air when the wall of water caught him within ten feet of safety, but the rest of the crew escaped.

The raging torrent struck the great fires at the Cambria Ironworks and the plant exploded. Seventy feet of water surged over the helpless city of Johnstown. Houses, bridges and buildings of every kind collapsed and carried their human burden to death. Within five minutes, more than two thousand persons had lost their lives, human sacrifices to the halfway measures which had been used at Conemaugh dam, victims of the heartless gods of haste and carelessness.

Flying Saucers and the Brass Curtain

ON June 19, 1956, the *Washington Evening Star* said in a front-page headline: 'Mystery Object Sighted Over Nation's Capital.'

The story dealt with the appearance over Washington of another Unidentified Flying Object, sighted by Ground Observer Corps watchers as it approached the National Airport, where it hovered for a few minutes glowing brightly, then sped away and vanished.

Officially it became another in the long series of unidentified flying objects which have been recorded over the nation's capital in recent years. Singly and in swarms they come, circling, swerving, hovering by turns. When jets are sent up to pursue them, they flip up on edge and race away, leaving the jets far behind.

What are they? Where do they come from? How do they operate? Why are they here?

But first—are they real?

The Air Force, which is entrusted with defending the nation against any and all aerial intruders, has since 1947 been conducting an extensive and expensive investigation of these phenomena popularly known as 'flying saucers'. The Air Force has followed a most extraordinary policy in its public statements on the matter, a policy of contradiction, confusion and perhaps of deception.

While the Air Force was solemnly assuring the public that those who reported these unidentified flying objects were sadly mistaken, the same Air Force was also spending huge sums of money trying to capture one of the very objects whose existence it denied.

While the Air Force persistently brushed aside such reports as 'mere hallucinations'—it was also sending up its fastest jet fighter planes to chase the 'hallucinations'!

Each year, as the Air Force announced that it was closing its latest project of investigating these unidentified aerial objects, it neglected to add that it was opening another such project immediately, under a different name.

Perhaps this peculiar official policy was well founded. Perhaps there is developing a situation which warrants keeping the facts from the public as long as possible.

Let us examine the records.

Are the flying saucers real?

The answer to that question is a well-kept secret, if we expect an answer in so many words. But if we look about us we can arrive at a conclusion without being told. Fifteen major nations, including our own and Russia, have official government projects devoted to the study of the so-called flying saucers. Only France, of all the major countries, has no government agency in this field. And only in France are reports of sightings printed in their entirety as they occur.

The German saucer-study project was headed by Dr. Herman Oberth, famed rocket expert and long-time exponent of space travel. Dr. Oberth said, in June, 1955, that the studies of his group had convinced him that the flying saucers did not originate on this earth, but evidently came from somewhere out in space. (A few weeks later Dr. Oberth was brought to the U.S.A. and placed on the staff at Redstone Arsenal in Alabama, effectively terminating his public statements on the subject of unidentified flying objects.)

The British government followed a policy of free and public discussion on its findings in this field until the late summer of 1954, when it suddenly reversed itself and ordered all military and government personnel to make no further public statements dealing with unidentified flying objects.

Are the flying saucers real?

On May 15th, 1954, Air Force Chief of Staff General Nathan Twining was speaking in Amarillo, Texas. He said to his audience: 'The best brains in the Air Force are trying to solve this riddle [of the flying saucers]. If they come from Mars, they are so far ahead of us we have nothing to be afraid of.'

A few weeks after General Twining's remarkable statement at Amarillo, Colonel Frank Milani, Director of the Civil Defence Centre in Baltimore, publicly demanded that the Air Force end its 'policy of secrecy' on the U.F.O.s and tell the public what was happening.

Milani was referring to the numerous sightings which had been reported in the heavily populated area in which his group operated. The *Wilmington* (Delaware) *Morning News* for July 9, 1954, finally broke the story after the Air Force sought to muffle Milani's demands. Said the Wilmington paper in a front-page story: '100 Mystery Objects Sighted Here.'

The article quoted the Ground Observer Corps for its authority, since the G.O.C. people had made the sightings and reported them to the Baltimore Filter Centre. The sightings had extended over a two-year period, but the policy of official secrecy had prevented the public from knowing that these things, whatever they were, had been manœuvring around in the skies over Wilmington, watched by radar and by ground observers, and pursued vainly by jet interceptors. At least one of these objects, according to the official records, was of tremendous size, hovering at an altitude of many miles over the nation's capital before it moved towards Baltimore. It was listed in the records as an Unidentified Flying Object, which is the Air Force name for flying saucers!

Are they real?

The United States government evidently thinks they are, for the Pentagon issued two specific orders dealing with them. The first is known as JANAP 146-B CIRVIS. The word CIRVIS is formed from the initials of the title of the order—'Communicating Instructions for Reporting Vital Intelligence Sightings from Aircraft.' It was issued by the Joint Chiefs of Staff in September,

1951. It covered all military and civilian personnel under the jurisdiction of the government, ordering them to report immediately any sightings of *'unidentified flying objects'*.

That was a move that was made in 1951, before the mantle of secrecy had been fully lowered. In August of 1954, after Colonel Milani's demand for the publication of the facts and after the publication of the Wilmington reports, the second order was issued. Known as Air Force Regulation 200-2, this came from the Secretary of the Air Force. It stated flatly that it was concerned with unidentified flying objects (flying saucers)—'First as a possible threat to the security of the United States and its forces, and secondly, to determine technical aspects involved.'

In paragraph 9 of this order AFR 200-2, the Secretary of the Air Force gave specific instructions that reports of unidentified flying objects are *not* to be released. . . . 'Only reports . . . where the object has been definitely identified as a familiar object.'

The effect of these two official orders, JANAP 146-B and AFR 200-2, was to require immediate reporting of all sightings of strange objects in the air, and once those reports had been made, the persons involved were expressly forbidden to make any public statements.

What kind of reports had the public been getting?

It got one from the Air Force press desk at the Pentagon on June 10th, 1954, when the Air Force announced that flying saucers were on the wane because it had received only eighty-seven sighting reports in the first five months of the year.

The public got another jolt on that same night, when Colonel John O'Mara, Deputy Commander of Intelligence at Air Technical Intelligence Centre, Dayton, Ohio, told newsmen that 'the Air Force is now receiving more than seven hundred sighting reports per week—the highest rate in the history of the entire investigation'.

While the Air Force was getting its wire crossed in this fashion, hundreds of local newspapers were front-paging sighting reports by credible local citizens.

On May 17, 1954, the *Dallas Times-Herald* said, 'Four Jet Pilots Report Race With Saucers Over Dallas.'

The paper quoted veteran Marine Reserve pilot Major Charles Scarbrough, who was in command of the flight of four SF-97 jets. He told how he and his three companions suddenly found themselves in the midst of a flight of sixteen silvery, disc-shaped objects which played tag around the jets for several minutes, while the jets tried vainly to match the manœuvres of their eerie playmates.

The *Joliet* (Illinois) *News-Herald* said on that same day, 'Saucer Pays a Visit'—and it told how local citizens had watched a single silvery disc perform over the city.

From Alaska, from Uganda, Africa, from every state in the Union and from the countries of South America, the reports appeared. Whatever they were, they were being watched in all parts of the world.

But what were they?

Dr. Herman Oberth, who had identified them as visitors from space, was, by mid 1954, an employee of the United States government, subject to strict security regulations (including AFR 200-2) and could make no more public statements.

British Air Marshal Lord Dowding was a man with a distinguished military record and he was also a man who knew what was in the files of the British Royal Air Force. He said, in 1954, 'The flying saucers are unquestionably interplanetary craft and should be treated as such.'

Lord Dowding was not alone in his views that the saucers should be treated with extreme caution. In July of 1952, when scores of these strange objects sailed around over Washington, D.C., the jittery Air Force issued an order to its pursuit pilots— 'Shoot them down!' The order was issued shortly after noon on July 26, 1952, and it got nationwide coverage on the news wires as a matter of course. Prominent scientists, including the late Dr. Albert Einstein, called the White House to urge that the order be withdrawn in the interests of common sense. Their reasoning was logic itself: any intelligence able to cross space would be able to defend itself after it reached its goal, certainly against such comparatively primitive weapons as rockets and guns.

The 'shoot-'em-down' order was rescinded by White House orders shortly before five o'clock in the afternoon. That night, while Washington observers watched the objects on radar and with the naked eye, jets raced back and forth in pursuit. The objects sped away; the jets returned without a shot being fired.

Are the flying saucers real?

Even after this remarkable experience in Washington, the Air Force doggedly insisted that the things were nothing more than 'hallucinations'.

Did the Air Force really believe that?

In December, 1953, Colonel D. M. Blakeslee was flying an F-84 Thunderjet over northern Japan, when he spied before him in the gathering gloom a cluster of glowing objects. As he tried to close in on them with his jet operating at full throttle, Colonel Blakeslee reported that he could see the glowing objects flying in spiral formation around a common centre at the same time that they easily outdistanced him.

According to the Air Force 'explanation', Colonel Blakeslee was having a hallucination, but it is worth noting that he was not grounded for a single minute.

Lieutenant David Brigham, flying a P-51, was approaching his base in northern Japan on the night of March 29, 1952—sky clear, visibility excellent—when a shiny, disc-shaped thing came streaking in at him, came to a sudden stop in mid-air, then played around over his wings, cockpit and tail planes before it zoomed away from him. Another pilot, coming in behind him, also saw and verified the report.

If the Air Force believed its own 'explanation', both these fliers were in a bad way mentally, having 'hallucinations'. Neither man was grounded, of course.

The experiences of Lt. Brigham and Colonel Blakeslee are typical of those reported by hundreds of pilots, both military and commercial. It is worthy of note that *not a single pilot was ever grounded for having what the Air Force claims are 'hallucinations' of this sort!*

Is there a veil of censorship which has kept the public from being fully informed on these strange objects?

From 1947, when the so-called flying saucers first burst on the world news scene, until July of 1952, when they appeared in swarms over Washington, D.C., there was no consistent attempt to censor the publication of sightings on a national scale. But after July 26, 1952, and the commotion which attended the 'shoot-'em-down' order, the muzzle of censorship was clamped on.

For example: The July 20th and July 26th sightings over Washington involved a total of about forty unidentified flying objects. These sightings were widely reported in broadcasts and newspapers. But on August 13th, 1952, according to the official records of the Civil Aeronautics Administration, sixty-eight unidentified flying objects were visually sighted and tracked by radar within ten miles of the Washington National Airport in a three-hour period starting at 8.30 p.m. Although this group far outnumbered the widely publicized sightings of the preceding month, *not a word leaked out to the public through the muzzle of official censorship!* Disclosure of the amazing sightings of August 13th, 1952, finally leaked out through publication of a C.A.A. booklet in 1954 which instructed government personnel how to identify and track U.F.O.s.

As an example of how the censorship worked this incident is typical:

At ten minutes past midnight, October 19, 1953, a National Airlines DC-6 just out of Philadelphia en route for Washington was at 8,000 feet over the Conowingo Dam. The pilot had just reported his position and estimated arrival time. He hung up the microphone and settled back for a routine milk run to the National Airport.

Thirty seconds later he found himself confronted with a possible mid-air collision. A shiny, disc-shaped object slid out of a thin layer of clouds and came rushing at him. The co-pilot flipped on the wing lights as a warning. In return the object sent a blinding beam of white light into the cockpit of the airliner. The pilot, with only a few seconds left, threw the big DC-6 into a dive at full power. The object that had almost rammed them shot past overhead and vanished.

The commercial airliner had dropped to three thousand feet before it could be brought out of the dive. Passengers were piled in the aisles—the sudden manœuvre had caught them unprepared and tumbled them about. A radio call went out to have ambulances and doctors at the National Airport. Fortunately, this was a flight that arrived at a time when the airport was nearly deserted and, even more fortunately, none of the passengers was injured beyond a few bumps and scratches.

The story of this Unidentified Flying Object that apparently tried to ram a commercial airliner loaded with passengers appeared in the *Washington Post* next morning. It ran in only one edition. Then it was yanked out, and *it did not appear in any other paper, nor did it appear on any news wire*—although such an incident was front-page news.

Plugging the loopholes through which such incidents got national coverage must have been simplicity itself. All newspapers and most broadcasters rely for such coverage on the three news wire services: United Press, International News Service, Associated Press. If the news services do not carry the story, then it gets little or no publicity. The news services themselves are highly competitive and therefore highly vulnerable. They get scoops and tips and special material from the government, especially from the Pentagon, when it pleases the various agency heads to dole out their favours. The news agency which refused to co-operate (that is, which insisted on printing reports which the military wanted to suppress) would soon find itself being left out of many other stories which its competitors would get in return for their 'co-operation'. When the military decided to muzzle the distribution of flying saucer reports, the procedure involved two simple steps: First, a statement from the Air Force ridiculing the 'saucers'. The news wires dutifully carried this statement. It gave them an official peg on which to predicate their subsequent silence on

N

incidents which the military wanted suppressed. The second step in the suppression campaign involved an informal meeting with representatives of the three news services. . . . 'If you will just forget about the flying saucers, we will give you plenty of other stories in their place.'

Net result—after the startling sightings around Washington in mid-summer of 1952, there was the subsequent 'ridiculing' statement from the Air Force and the 'saucer' stories vanished from the news wires.

No such move was made, however, to muzzle local newspapers or local broadcasters. That would have been too risky—too many people involved—and besides, local publicity never had any effect outside the range of the broadcasting station or the newspaper which used the story. This is why hundreds of newspapers each year have carried reports of local sightings by credible witnesses, but with few exceptions these reports are not reprinted elsewhere.

It is evident from the record that these mysterious objects are not 'hallucinations' even in the minds of those who officially profess to dismiss them as such. It is equally clear that in many nations, including our own, there is a continuous and continuing programme of investigation aimed at acquiring every bit of information that has a bearing on these objects. The record also shows that the 'flying saucers' which are discredited by the Air Force are identical to the unidentified flying objects with which some of the largest branches of our military are deeply engrossed. The things have been observed and reported by credible witnesses in every part of the world. They have been photographed. They have been watched through astronomers' telescopes and tracked on radar screens. They have been (and still are) chased by jet pursuit planes when such pursuit is practicable.

That much is common knowledge, but it leaves many vital questions unanswered.

Where do these things originate? What do they want? Do they (as Dr. Oberth and others suspect) power themselves by distortion of the gravitational field? Is there any significance in the fact that the number of sightings increases greatly in the years when the earth and Mars are in their closest approach? If these things do come from another planet, are they using the moon for a base from which to survey the earth and its inhabitants? Does this explain the strange lights and changes which astronomers have reported on the moon in recent years?

When and *if* the answers to those questions filter through the curtain of official secrecy, the world will have the answer to the riddle of the flying saucers.

In the meantime, the depth of the enigma is accentuated by the remarkable statement of General Douglas MacArthur, who said in an interview on December 7, 1955: 'The nations of the world will be forced to unite. . . . for the next war will be an interplanetary war.'

Signals from Space

ARE beings on other planets trying to communicate with us?

Radio signals from outer space are not new, but our ability to receive and identify them has improved vastly since such things were first reported.

On June 4, 1956, the Naval Observatory in Washington announced that its scientists had succeeded in making what was believed to be the first 'radio contact' with Venus. The report stated that several weak signals from Venus had been picked up and identified by the giant radio-telescopes at the Naval Research Laboratories in Washington. From the nature and characteristics of the signals received, it was deduced that Venus has a surface temperature about the boiling point of water, which, if correct, would help to explain why that planet is surrounded by a thick blanket of steam or gas.

Ohio State University released a Press statement on July 2, 1956, which went a bit further than that of the Naval Observatory. It stated that on June 22nd an Ohio State University radio astronomer, Dr. John D. Kraus, had received radio signals 'of a type resembling radio telegraphy in many ways', and these signals, said the University, came from a source presumed to be Venus.

Dr. Kraus reported that he was actually receiving two distinct types of radio signals from out in space. Since June 1st he had been picking up strong crackling or 'Class One' signals on a wavelength of 11 metres. But in addition to this Class One type (sometimes originated by terrestrial thunderstorms) Dr. Kraus had also been receiving for about two months signals of a distinctly different type: 'Class Two' signals, which he said presumably originate on Venus.

These signals were received only when the giant radio-telescope at Ohio State University was trained precisely on Venus. Dr. Kraus suspected that these Class Two signals, 'which have many of the characteristics of signals of a terrestrial radio transmitting station', might be nothing more than freak interference from some station on earth. After sufficiently numerous and varied observations, however, Dr. Kraus came to the conclusion that it was 'very likely that they do come from Venus'. Certainly they came along with the Class One signals, and they came only when the planet was directly in the beam of the radio-telescope.

This is by no means an isolated case or experience.

Great observatories and universities all over the world are installing radio-telescopes—huge metallic dishes which can be focussed on individual planets, just as Dr. Kraus pinpointed Venus with the radio-telescope at Ohio State University. These devices are very sensitive. They are also very costly, and their purchase and use is no mere happenstance. They are there for a purpose—*to discover if intelligent beings out in space are signalling.*

This is really only the latest development in a story that began around the turn of the century, when Marconi reported that he was picking up signals on a frequency not being used by any terrestrial transmitter. Listening on his yacht in the Mediterranean, Marconi detected signals which he regarded as code, meaningless to him. He instructed one of his assistants to make a public statement on the matter at a forthcoming speech to some New York business men. The assistant read Marconi's telegram to the audience, there was a brief flurry of excitement in the feature sections of the Sunday papers, then the matter was quietly dropped.

Nikola Tesla, famed Yugoslav electrical wizard, also reported receiving cryptic code signals which seemed to be most numerous and strong when his antenna was directed towards Mars. Tesla, like Marconi, had no qualms about making his findings public. If Mars was trying to reach us, these men thought we should know about it.

In 1924, radio engineers announced that they, too, had picked up these mysterious chatterings which did not conform to any known code, but which seemed to be intelligently conceived and directed. The signals received by them were recorded, discussed, then filed and forgotten.

But not for long. Scarcely more than a year after this incident, scientists in the Naval Research Laboratories in Washington came in for a surprise. They were testing a process for recording wireless signals on film. Out of the ether came a weird chirping which made no sense in terms of understandable code, but when the film was developed the scientists were astounded to find that the signals had arrived in such fashion that they recorded in the form of faces! Caricatures, to be sure, but faces beyond a doubt.

And in 1926, after many months of preparation, the scientists from Johns Hopkins University, along with radio experts from both the Signal Corps and the Navy, were ready to try to contact Mars. They had spent hundreds of thousands of dollars building powerful transmitting equipment and delicate receivers in Nebraska. Their efforts lasted about two weeks and, according to the statements released to the public at the termination of the tests, came to naught.

Thirty years later, science is again listening for signals from Mars or Venus—with better equipment this time, and apparently with better results.

The chronicle of mysterious broadcasts would not be complete without one which is certainly strangest of all, and perhaps most significant in the final analysis.

Television is relatively restricted in its range. A station with a coverage area of one hundred and fifty miles radius is fortunate indeed. That is why television viewers in England were startled to see on their screens in September of 1953 the station identification card and call letters of television station KLEE in Houston, Texas. The signals came in strong throughout a large portion of the British Isles, so strong that many viewers had ample time to photograph this remarkable long-range television reception. British broadcast engineers were promptly informed of the unusual circumstances and they too were able to pick up the signal without difficulty.

Freak long-range television pickups are rather more common than the public realizes and the British authorities attached no real importance to this reception of the KLEE signal, at least not until they contacted KLEE on the matter. Then they got a real surprise!

KLEE, Houston, Texas, went off the air in 1950. The successor to KLEE informed the British Broadcasting Corporation that no KLEE identification card had been televised at any time since 1950—three years before the signals were picked up in Britain!

The British finally decided that it was a matter which defied analysis. For someone to have broadcast that signal as a practical joke would have meant expenditure of at least one hundred thousand dollars, as well as involving considerable risk and requiring special equipment. The chances that it was a pointless practical joke were ruled out by both British and American authorities.

What did happen? Where did the signal come from? Why was KLEE chosen for the broadcast, when it had not been on the air for three years? Why were the signals beamed only to the British Isles? Who sent them?

A chief engineer for the British Broadcasting Corporation told newsmen: 'We are confronted in this instance with a set of circumstances which are at variance with accepted knowledge of television transmission. It is unthinkable that these signals could have been circling the earth for the period of time since that station last broadcast them. It is physically impossible that they

could have been reflected to us by chance from any celestial body
at such a vast distance. That leaves us with but one possibility,
however bizarre: that these signals were transmitted to us purpose-
fully and intelligently, frרn a source and for a purpose presently
unknown.'

The Devil in Devon

ON the snowy morning of February 8, 1855, the good folks of Devonshire, England, awoke to find that they had played host to a mysterious visitor during the night. From Topsham and Bicton in the north to Dawlish and Totnes in the south, something had scampered, or pranced, or slithered, over fences and fields, over walls and housetops, leaving thousands of footprints in an unbroken line to mark its passing.

What was it, this thing that could travel up the walls and over the rooftops of decent, God-fearing folks while they slept? Where did it come from—and where did it go?

Early on that eventful evening there had been a heavy fall of snow in Devonshire. A great unblemished white mat had been spread on which this strange visitor could leave a record of his passing. And with the coming of daylight the message came to notice.

It is quite possible that several persons discovered the trail at different points almost simultaneously. However that may be, we do know that a baker in Topsham, one George Fairly, noticed the strange marks which preceded him to the door of his little shop. From a point about three feet short of the door the tracks turned abruptly right and followed along a five-foot-high brick wall for a few feet. There they vanished—just stopped short in the snow.

Mr. Fairly looked around for some hint to the next move of his early morning visitor.

He noticed that the snow which curled softly over the top of the wall was disturbed, and upon examination he found that the creature which had made the footprints along the base of the wall had somehow leaped up on top of it and walked along for some distance before taking to earth again, the single row of little hoof-shaped marks trailing across the field towards the bay. Mr. Fairly was mildly curious, but he was not deeply concerned or alarmed. He had baking to do.

In other communities in Devonshire that morning, others were making the same sort of discovery that the baker of Topsham had made. Something had crossed through the countryside during the night, evidently after the snowfall had ceased, around eleven o'clock. The creature had left a single line of small tracks in the snow. Variously described as hoof-prints, crescents and broken oblongs, the marks followed a course more than a hundred miles long, from Exmouth by the sea, north to Raleigh and Bicton, west to Woodbury and Topsham and then to the water's edge, reappearing on the south shore of the inlet at Powdersham, then meandering to Luscombe, Dawlish and Teignmouth. There, again at the water's edge, the tracks vanished, to reappear several miles away on the south shore near Newton, then at Torquay, and from there, over rooftops and fences and snowy fields, to Totnes. Unfortunately for subsequent investigation, no effort was made to determine where the tracks went from Totnes, if they went any-where.

By mid-morning the countryside was aroused and excited. Groups of men armed themselves with anything that came handy and set out to seek the creature of such fantastic capabilities which had left its marks on their homes and doorsteps during the preceding night. As is customary in such cases, rumours flew and gossip grew until by mid-afternoon a state of near panic was in full swing among the ignorant and unstable.

But there were others on the scene, and it is to them that we are indebted for the facts which put this case in the records. For the most part these were local citizens of good standing who covered the story for the London newspapers, of which *The Times* carried the most complete accounts.

Under the headline 'Extraordinary Circumstances', *The Times* carried its first article on February 16, 1855, in which it stated that there had been great excitement throughout that section of Devonshire where some strange creature of remarkable powers had left its footprints in the snow on rooftops, fences and in courtyards enclosed by high fences.

Said *The Times*:

> 'The track appeared more like that of a biped than a quadruped, and the steps were generally eight inches in advance of each other. The impressions of feet closely resembled those of a donkey's shoe, and measured from an inch and a half to (in some instances) two and a half inches across. Here and there it appeared as if cloven, but in the generality of the steps the shoe was continuous, and from the snow in the centre remaining entire, merely showing the outer crest of the foot, it must have been convex.'

The Times reporter noted that the creature had approached the doors of many homes and had retreated without giving any impression which would indicate that it had paused to rest. Eight days after the event the newspapers reported that there was still so much excitement about the matter that many persons were afraid to leave their homes at night except in armed groups.

From the evidence of many reports and many reporters it is possible to assemble a rather complete picture of what happened, except that there is still no answer to the most important question of all—what made the mystery footprints of Devonshire?

The trail began near the sea at Exmouth and followed the course already specified, through fields and forests, hamlets and towns. For more than a hundred miles the little tracks ran on and on. Where they could be plainly seen under good circumstances they were uniform in appearance: U-shaped marks about four inches long, spaced slightly more than eight inches apart. Oddly, they ran in a straight line, one exactly before the other, mile after mile. If the marks were made by a quadruped it was a most unusual creature for this reason alone. And no biped, with the exception of some birds, sets its feet down in a ruler-straight line as it ambles along.

In the midst of any such excitement it is inevitable that local 'experts' appear with 'explanations'. In the case of the strange footprints of Devonshire, various gentlemen came forward with divers answers. The Reverend G. M. Musgrave was among the first to 'solve' the mystery. He blandly assured his nervous parishioners that the footprints had been made by nothing more mysterious than a kangaroo. This left another facet of the matter unexplained, however, for there were no kangaroos in Devonshire—even had one been capable of travelling over rooftops.

Other 'experts' basked briefly in the limelight with their solemn assertions that they had examined the prints and found them to be the work of badgers, otters, kangaroo rats or huge birds alien to that part of the world. All these proffered solutions had the same basic fault—they failed to meet the existing circumstances. The thing that had left its tracks from Exmouth to Totnes had crossed two large bodies of very cold water. It had gone under low bushes without knocking the snow off them. It had leaped nimbly from earth to rooftops and had pursued its course along the tops of narrow walls and uneven fence palings. And, most baffling of all, it had done these things in a remarkably short space of time, for it was less than five hours between the time the snowfall stopped and baker Fairly's discovery of the prints around his shop. Whatever it was that made the footprints had made them with unusual rapidity to have covered so much territory in such a short space of time.

Investigators advanced the theory that two (or possibly three) creatures of unknown type might have been involved. One, they postulated, had come out of the Exe River at Exmouth, roamed through Bicton and Topsham and had then gone back into the bay. The other, according to this theory, had come out of the bay near Powderham Castle and made the journey to Teignmouth, where it again took to the water. And by this same line of reasoning, still a third creature left the inlet at Teignmouth and roamed afield to the end of the trail at Totnes. This theory is credible if you wish to assume that three creatures of unknown type were possessed by the same irresistible urge at the same time in the same place: to come out of the sea at three different spots on the coast of Devonshire on the same night, pursuing their meandering courses over fields and rooftops and scurrying back into the water, never to be seen or heard of again. But by dividing the line of tracks into three segments, the theory at least possessed the virtue of slowing down the pace of the creature involved, whatever it was.

Several thousand persons saw the footprints before a change in the weather obliterated them. There was general agreement that the tracks were small, hoof-shaped indentations, uniform in size and presentation throughout the area over which they were distributed. Gradually the excitement died down, and the puzzling footprints ceased to be a major topic of conversation. Such things had never before been seen in Devonshire and have never been seen since, at least there.

Similar marks, however, have been recorded elsewhere. As a matter of fact the Devonshire Devil may have had a predecessor in the Antarctic in May, 1840, when, according to the noted polar explorer Captain James C. Ross, he made a landing on a barren spot known as Kerguelen Island, on the fringes of the Antarctic. In his official account of the matter Captain Ross wrote:

'Of land animals we saw none; and the only traces we could discover of there being any on this island were the singular footprints of a pony or ass, found by the party detached for surveying purposes, under the command of Lieutenant Bird, and described by Dr. Robertson as being three inches in length and two and a half in breadth, having a small and deeper depression on each side and shaped like a horseshoe. . . . They traced its footsteps for some distance in the recently fallen snow, in hopes of getting sight of it, but lost the tracks on reaching a large space of rocky ground which was free from snow.'

Whatever it was, the Kerguelen creature resembled that of Devonshire in two important respects: it made tracks like a small pony and it made them in snow without being observed by human beings.

Do such things exist in the oceans, along the edges of which these strange footprints were found? Admittedly we know very little about the denizens of the deep, but occasionally we get a peep at some of the fantastic creatures which abide there, as for instance in November of 1953 when a most unusual thing washed ashore at Canvey Island, England. Badly decomposed, it resembled nothing the authorities had ever seen before, because it appeared to be some sort of marine creature with feet and legs so arranged that it could walk upright. After the learned men had completed their examinations without arriving at any public conclusions, the enigma was cremated.

Unfortunately for the perplexed authorities, the case did not end there. On August 11, 1954, the Reverend Joseph Overs was strolling along the beach at Canvey Island when he came upon a grotesque carcass wallowing in a small tidal pool. The gentleman sent one of his youngsters for the police. The bobbies pulled the carcass ashore and sent for the experts.

The creature which had washed ashore there the preceding November had been about two and a half feet long—or tall, as the case may be. But this latest arrival was slightly more than four feet in length, weighed about twenty-five pounds and was in good condition for examination. The report shows that it had two large eyes, nostril holes and below that a gaping mouth. It had gills, but instead of scales the thing was covered with pink skin which the doctors found to be as tough as that of a hog. Most remarkable of all, this creature, like that of the preceding November, had two short legs with perfect feet—feet which ended in five little toes, arranged in a U-shape with a concave centre arch.

Did these strange creatures point to a solution to the riddle of the Devonshire footprints of a century before—or did they merely add new question marks to compound the mystery?